ABC's of Grief

A Handbook for Survivors

Christine A. Adams

Second Edition- Reprint

ISBN: 10 154052595
ISBN 13: 978-1540525291

Published by Create Space - 2017

First Edition Information: 2003 - Library of Congress Catalog Number: 2003044446
ISBN: 0-89503-243-0 (paper)

Baywood Publishing Company, Inc.
Amityville, NY 11701

Library of Congress Cataloging-in-Publication Data
Adams, Christine A.
ABC's of grief: a handbook for survivors / Christine A. Adams,
p. cm.
Includes bibliographical references and index.
ISBN 0-89503-243-0 (pbk.)
1. Grief-Dictionaries. 2. Bereavement-Psychological aspects-Dictionaries. 3. Death-Psychological aspects-Dictionaries. I. Title.

BF575.G7A32 2003
155.9'37-dc21
2003044446

Author photo by Marilee Frazier?

Dedication

This Book is dedicated to
The McKenna Family

My parents:
Martin Michael McKenna
Bridie Mary McKenna

My sisters:
Mary and Eileen

My brothers:
Michael, John, and David

And especially to
My brother Daniel P. McKenna

To Robert McKenna
With love,

Christine

Table of Contents

CHAPTER 5: E

CHAPTER 6: F

CHAPTER 7: G

CHAPTER 8: H

CHAPTER 9: I

CHAPTER 10: J

CHAPTER 11: K

CHAPTER 12: L

CHAPTER 13: M

Acknowledgments

To all those who made this book possible, a heartfelt thank-you! Each one of you helped make this Handbook available to those who grieve.

To the poets and writers who shared so generously.

To Mr. Stuart Cohen, The President of Baywood Publishing Co., Inc.

To John D. Morgan, Ph.D., Baywood's editor of the *Death, Value and Meaning Series*

To Baywood's production and editorial personnel, Bobbi Olszewski and Julie Krempa.

To my husband Robert J. Butch and my children Edward, Marcia, and Mark, and my stepsons Tom, Bob, and Bill.

To my teacher and mentor, Virginia W. Parsons

Introduction

The *ABC's of Grief: A Handbook for Survivors* is a book that meets the grieving person wherever they might be in their process. The object of this book is to provide snatches of meaning, hope, empathy, and understanding captured within a comprehensive study of the many aspects of the grief process.

ABC's was never meant to be read cover to cover. Just skip around choosing any topic. The alphabetical format merely simplifies the book allowing a reader, or group leader, to focus on any aspect of grief that suits them. Each letter is designed to cover several problems. For example, **D** includes a discussion of both the early feelings of **Denial, Despair,** and later processes of **Discovery**. The words are not in any specific order other than they begin with D and relate to grief.

Most books dealing with grief, including sections of *ABC's of Grief,* explain discernable *stages of recovery*. Although this can be a useful format for writing, it can be misleading because no survivor experiences the process in the same way. And, rarely in a linear fashion! For example, we don't get over "the anger stage"; we sometimes slip back into anger many times along the way.

The flexibility within this book allows the survivor to live with his or her grief, go through the process, and not feel forced to get over it. If a reader gets stuck in their "anger" or "anxiety," they can go back to reread those parts of the book. Perhaps each time they go back they find some realization, some new meaning. In that way, *ABC's of Grief* could help the reader go deeper and possibly find their way out of the anger or anxiety.

Additionally, there's a difference between the early days of grief and a later time. Reading any comprehensive, structured book on the process of grief may prove too much for the grief stricken reader in the early days of shock, disorientation, and confusion. But they might be able to handle a poem written by someone who has also lost a loved one. Therefore, each section contains appropriate quotes, stories, and poems.

These quotes, stories, and poems are brought into the text to lend variety to the format, change the rhythm of the text, and put the reader in touch with a fellow survivor. Intentionally, most poems are not the words of renowned poets but survivors who found solace in writing a poem to describe their situation or honor their loved one. Storytellers who learned powerful lessons about death and life wrote the stories.

As the author of *ABC's of Grief,* I can only hope that this book will give to the reader what it has given me. *ABC's* was written over a three-year period because, like the reader, I needed to assimilate the material slowly so I wouldn't become lost in the heaviness of grief. Reading many of the poems and stories went right to my heart and brought me to tears. These tears helped me heal some unfinished portions of my own grief.

I found that grief patiently waits to be invited back into our lives; and sometimes, not so patiently can turn to apathy or a lingering anger. *ABC's of Grief* gives the survivor the message that it's OK to grieve at your own pace, there's no pattern. It's OK to release those uncried tears, there's no timetable. And when you embrace your grief, one day at a time, one thought, word, or letter at a time, you grow and heal.

CHAPTER 1

ABSENCE

There's no way to fill the void left by the one we loved. If our loved one was the center of our universe, now that center is removed. We long only for the loved one to come back and be alive in the world with us.

We developed rituals with our loved one—small routines. Now the absence of that habitual word or act creates a void. It may have been a phone call at a certain time of day, the bedtime story for a child, the hugs you always shared. Whatever it was, now that it's gone, you feel a small, painful stab when you notice the habit you've grown so used to is no longer there and realize it will never be experienced again.

When you feel the pain, the only solace is to remember and recognize the gift of having had such a relationship. What if you had never known a husband's love, the touch of a child, the warmth of a friendship?

Share the memories of the things you miss most with someone who knew your loved one, or someone who has lost a husband, child, or friend. Write in your journal, or write a poem. In "Honeysuckle Summer," Rosemary J. Gwaltney remembers, laments, and weeps.

Honeysuckle Summer

Fragrant the
Honeysuckle vines
Behind the back porch
Where we spent the summer
Swinging snugly in the gleaming

Moonlight. Barn owls calling urgently
Back and forth. We were lost in each other's
Smiles; hypnotized by each other's hands
Clasped together, in promises of spring.
Entwined in scented dreams sweeter
Than richest masses of blossoms
Twisting yellow through
The railing.

Who could have seen it coming?
The sentence of sickness
Descending.

When the first frost arrived
Lightly dusting pumpkins and squashes,
I lay alone between rows of dried cornstalks
In the field beyond the chicken-house,
Face down in the icy mud
Weeping.

AVOIDANCE

Although there's no definite pattern in the grieving process, three major phases of response to grief seem to emerge over and over again. The first, *avoidance,* is characterized by shock, denial, and disbelief; the second, *confrontation,* is a highly charged and emotional time which might start with anger and end in depression; the third, *accommodation,* is a time where there is a gradual decline of acute grief and the beginning of an emotional and social reentry into the everyday world.

In the *avoidance phase,* that period of time in which the news of death is initially received, you desire to avoid the terrible acknowledgment that the person you loved is now deceased. A survivor may find himself or herself thinking:

I can't believe it! John cannot be dead!

You've made a mistake. Officer, this is not my daughter.

I cannot feel anything. This must be a dream.

Your world is shaken; you feel overwhelmed. Just as the human body goes into shock after a severe physical trauma, so too does the human psyche go into shock when confronted with such an important loss. It's the natural reaction to the impact of such a blow.

During this period you may respond in several ways. You may be confused and dazed, unable to comprehend what has happened. You may feel bewildered and numb. Disorganization is normal. You might stay in bed as a means of avoidance, or become hyperactive to avoid feeling at all.

At this point, avoidance might be therapeutic. It functions as a buffer by allowing you to absorb the reality of the loss a little at a time, rather than being completely overwhelmed by it. Avoiding the reality of the loss can be an emotional anesthesia that serves as a protective mechanism in the early days of grief.

You probably will continue to feel confused and disorganized until you are able to confront your feelings in the second phase. In the *confrontation phase* you may experience an outburst of emotion. This could be an explosion of anger, overwhelming sadness, hysteria, tears, rageful protest, or screaming. After this outburst of emotion, you may quietly withdraw, act mechanically without feeling, slipping into a depressed state. You might feel like you are living outside of your own body looking from a distance at what is happening to you.

Finally, in time there may be an *accommodation phase* where these acute feelings will ease. In this phase, you may experience a gradual decline of the acute sense of disorientation, and an awareness of your own avoidance and denial. You may be less prone to emotional twists and bursts of anger. In this period you may see the beginning of emotional and social reentry into everyday living.

Although three phases are sketched out here as a pattern, all survivors need to know their grief is unique. It may not follow any discernable pattern. You may never go through avoidance, or have outbursts of anger, or feel as though you have come to a place of accommodation. There is no prescriptive pattern in your grief process. Grief is not defined by its stages; grief is simply experienced individually.

In another poem by Rosemary J. Gwaltney, she speaks of her own sense of loss but also states that this poem "could speak for many different people, facing different kinds of losses."

What Can Be Said About Loss

What can be said about loss
In love—
Those gaping wounds bleeding from aching spirits.

Rich libraries of memories calling from those
Cob-webbed shelves of the mind, of empty
Arms, and absent laughter, loving ways,
Sparkling eyes no longer there. Of
Breakfast tables, lonely beds
And favorite things
Gathering
Dust.

What can be said about love
When loss
Rips the tapestry of a spirit apart, leaving threadbare
A soul unraveling. When child, friend, parent, or
Lover carries away with them irretrievably,
A central, vital piece of living. When
Nothing is ever the same again.
When healing takes so very
Long, leaving such
Hideous
Scars.

ANXIETY

There are many sources of anxiety associated with the grief process. First, we naturally hold back pain, yet knowing there is more pain we become fearful. Secondly, we deal with our insecurities, and become anxious over our emotional state. Thirdly, our concerns about our own emotional state set up further fears and anxieties.

1. Anticipating Pain Sets Up Fears

In early grief, we can feel only the "necessary pain," not the entire pain. It's as if our hearts and minds have a quota for emotional pain and nature protects us by allowing only that quota for this day, or the hour. When we can handle it, more will come. This natural tendency to hold back the pain can cause an inner anxiety.

Knowing that there's more emotional pain to be experienced sets up fears: the fear of losing control and falling apart, fear of not being able to function and do the things we need to do—like making decisions—and fear of causing others pain by our loss of control.

2. Dealing with Insecurities Causes Anxiety

By definition, any major loss always brings some insecurity, at least temporarily. This occurs naturally as you undergo the transition from the security of what was (having your loved one alive and present) to the insecurity of what is (being without the person who was such an important element in your life). This insecurity may become translated into a general feeling of "being unsettled." This kind of unsettling can make the survivor extremely anxious and even uncomfortable in their own skin.

3. Concerns About Your Emotional State May Further Increase Anxiety and Insecurity

Grief is like a rollercoaster ride of emotion, with foreign feelings and a confused sense of self. These combined with your natural wish to undo the death make it seem like a horrible nightmare. You try to fathom an incomprehensible situation. You ask, "How could the one I love so much have been taken from me?" It doesn't make any sense, and that only underscores your feelings of confusion and unreality.

You might find you have feelings of panic and anxiety when you awaken in the morning and remember you must face another day without the person who died. Many issues may trouble you and intensify these feelings:

- Concerns about going it alone
- Panic about being able to deal with the separation pain
- Fear about what the absence of your loved one will do to your life
- Worry over how the rest of your family is coping
- Fright arising from the sense of vulnerability caused by the loss
- Terror at the thought of losing others who are close to you
- Distress associated with your memories of earlier losses and separations
- Heightened emotional and physical arousal that exacerbates your feelings of tension and uneasiness

Recognizing that you have no power to prevent or undo the death of your loved one can cause you feelings of loss of control over your life and world. When the death is unanticipated, these feelings are intensified. You feel overwhelmed because your expectations of continuing on in life with the person you loved have been violated by that person's death. Also, the myth of your invulnerability has been shattered. Previously, you may have thought loss only happens to other people.

ANGER

Anger often displaces other feelings of hurt, fear, or despair that may be more difficult to confront. Using anger is like changing the subject when we are talking in order to evade the topic under discussion.

Anger can be dangerous if it's seeking a target—someone to blame for the loss, someone to confront. Anger seems to blur other activities and responsibilities that need to be looked at or attended to. Also, anger can be debilitating to our health, causing our general physical condition—which may be weakened by our grief—to erode even further.

When you are seized by anger, stop, take a few breaths, and ask yourself, "If I weren't angry now, what other feelings would I be having?" Anger is often a mask for other feelings and it's those feelings that deserve your attention and expression.

If you're angry because you're alone, you need to do something to break the cycle of loneliness. If you turn away from offers of help, friendship, and companionship, the bleak world you are creating will become even darker.

You can create a spark of light in your dark lonely world by responding to a friendly gesture, talking to a stranger, inviting someone to spend some time with you, making a phone call, or sending a note to a friend. As an old Chinese proverb says, "It is better to light a candle than curse the darkness."

Ed and His Father

Ed lost his father suddenly, without a chance to say good-bye to the man to whom he was so devoted. When he heard his father unexpectedly had become seriously ill, he sped from one state to the next trying to reach his father before it was too late.

However, after his mad rush he arrived at the hospital to find his father had died shortly before and his father's body had been removed moments prior to his walking into the room. Ed never had the opportunity to see or touch his beloved father until the wake.

In therapy, Ed spoke of how his Irish Catholic family wanted to focus on all the good memories they had of his father. Crying was regarded as inappropriate, since they believed it indicated a lack of faith. Anger was unheard of. Family members were supposed to assuage their grief and dismiss their feelings by focusing on the good times.

One day in therapy it became strikingly clear that Ed was absolutely furious over the death of his father and the lack of opportunity to say good-bye. When his therapist interpreted that he was angry, Ed found it impossible to accept. Somehow, he thought anger was inappropriate.

Ed then was asked how he would feel if his car were stolen while he was in the therapy session. He immediately responded that he would want to destroy the thief. He went on for several minutes in a heated tirade. When he calmed down, Ed was asked how he felt about his father being "stolen" from him.

At that moment he finally could recognize that while he could allow himself to be angry over the loss of his car, he had not permitted himself the same luxury over the loss of his father. The analogy assisted Ed in realizing the appropriateness of his angry response to the death of his father and to his being "robbed" of the farewell he desired.

ACCEPTING: A SPIRITUAL ANSWER

At first we may ask "why"? It's natural to question life and death. Yet, some of the most profound questions can only be explored and discussed. Some have no definitive answers. In the process of grief, we will be carried by faith. Faith seems to be the only antidote to obsessive questioning. Faith can carry the survivor to acceptance.

We associate having faith with a belief in God, and perhaps an afterlife. Grief may bring anger at God or the conviction that there's no God at all. Having lost that connection to a spiritual world makes it difficult for some people to accept death.

Others seem to get back to a spiritual place when they accept that their loved one is still with them in spirit. In time, a different understanding can arise when they realize that their loved one may not be sitting beside them, or coming through the door, but he or she is there just the same. Some believe the spirit of the person whose life they shared never dissolves, never departs, never desserts us.

Judy Burnette-Martin expresses this belief in her poetry. She feels that when someone we love dies, if we close our eyes, we can still see them in our everyday walk of life. She explains how the presence of her loved one was all around her in everything she did, and everywhere she would go.

Christmas From The Heart

I heard your voice in the wind today
and I turned to see your face;
The warmth of the wind caressed me
as I stood silently in place.

I felt your touch in the sun today
as its warmth filled the sky;
I closed my eyes for your embrace
and my spirit soared high.

I saw your eyes in the window pane
as I watched the falling rain;
It seemed as each raindrop fell
it quietly said your name.

I held you close in my heart today
it made me feel complete;
You may have died . . . but you are not gone
you will always be a part of me.

As long as the sun shines . . .
the wind blows . . .
the rain falls . . .
You will live on inside of me forever
For that is all my heart knows.

© by Judy Burnette-Martin

All sorrow comes to a time of acceptance. We don't need to hold so tightly, to live with the intense longing, to live in the void left by the absence of the one we loved. It may be true that the death came too soon, like the loss of a child, or may have come in a terrible way, like a vicious murder. But still, eventually, although we never forget, we accept the death into our life.

Judy Burnette further explains how she feels about her Dad's death "My dad died suddenly with a heart attack when I was 22. No matter the days that have past, I can still feel him nearby and there are times that I miss him so. As long as he lives in my memory, he will always be close by."

Dad

Dad . . . so many images come to mind
whenever I speak your name;
It seems without you in my life
things have never been the same.
What happened to those lazy days
when I was just a child;
When my life was consumed in you
in your love, and in your smile.

What happened to all those times
when I always looked to you;
No matter what happened in my life
you could make my gray skies blue.

Dad, some days I hear your voice
and turn to see your face;
Yet in my turning . . . it seems
the sound has been erased.

Dad, who will I turn to for answers
when life does not make sense;
Who will be there to hold me close
when the pieces just don't fit.

Oh, Dad, if I could turn back time
and once more hear your voice;
I'd tell you that out of all the dads
you would still be my choice.

Please always know I love you
and no one can take your place;
Years may come and go
but your memory will never be erased.

Today, Jesus, as You are listening
in your home above;
Would you go and find my dad
and give him all my love.

© by Judy Burnette-Martin

CHAPTER 2

BELIEF

If there seems to be no reason why your loved one died, especially in the case of a tragic loss or the death of a child, the death itself may seem like a punishment. It's not. When we feel punished, it's hard to maintain faith in a loving God.

Faith implies that we accept that some things are beyond our understanding. Giving up on God means we're giving up on the love God offers us. Life may have dealt us a cruel blow, but God is not a punishing being. God is Love, Itself.

Whenever we're hurt, we lose our sense of trust. We can't trust that we will be able to conduct our lives again; we wonder if tragedy will return to us. Sometimes it's hard even to trust other people, and specifically God—a force greater than ourselves.

If this death has shaken your faith, you can return to a place of trust by slowly renewing faith in others and in the community that surrounds you. By believing in people, you can renew your belief in God because God seems to work through the love of others.

At first, it may be impossible to return to a full life because all trust is gone. With time, and a conscious recognition that you're not being punished, you can resume a full life knowing you are loved and that life is worth living.

In this amazing story first published by Centering Corporation in their Caring Concepts Newsletter (1991), Marly Hayer talks about how her faith was restored by an unusual spiritual experience:

> It had been three months since a terrible triple tragedy had befallen us. Our two oldest sons, along with the lovely young girl our eldest

had planned to marry, had all died in a house fire at Eastern Illinois University. We were still suffering from shock, incredible grief, and disbelief. Somehow, we managed to go through the motions of the holidays. Now the New Year was here. Reality was sinking in. We could hardly stand to think of the rest of our lives without our boys. They were honor students, star athletes, and good and loving sons. We were at our lowest ebb.

The night of January 18 was cold and crisp. The stars were bright when I went out for a walk. As I made my way through the darkness, I thought constantly of the three we loved and missed so much. I walked and talked aloud, cried and tried to pray, but it seemed all my former faith and trust were gone. I felt as if I could not go on any longer unless I could be assured that they were all right.

Soon I could not tell if I was shaking from sobs or the cold. I felt as if I just had to know they were safe and happy somewhere. I realized I was freezing cold and utterly exhausted. As I turned to walk back toward the house, something off to the side of the road caught my eye. A bright light seemed to be moving toward me on the left. It was like a very large star. It was low, at the level of the treetops, traveling parallel to the road. It was moving very slowly on a straight path, and not at all like any falling star I had ever seen.

I watched in awe as it kept steadily moving toward me. Then, just as it was directly across and above the spot where I stood, it stopped and broke into three separate stars. They disappeared as quickly as they had come.

I was suddenly convinced, beyond a shadow of a doubt, that Bob, Mike, and Carla were with God. I began sensing a peace I had not known for months. A million stars seemed to close in around me. I was overwhelmed with a tremendous feeling of warmth and love and began to weep tears of joy.

My faith was restored. I'm forever grateful for that symbol of light in my darkness. There is no more fear or doubt in my life. Only an unshakable trust that, someday, we will be reunited with our loved ones for all eternity (by Marly Hayer).

BURDEN

Grief is a heavy burden but it's a burden that serves as a proof that we have the ability to gain closeness with another, to feel affection, and to dedicate part of our energy and emotion to another. It proves we have the capacity to love.

So why do we have to live through the terrible burden of grief? If you never experience love, then there would be no involvement that would be strong enough to cause unpleasant emotions. Even though the road you're traveling is difficult, would you give up the love you have experienced to avoid the pain? Probably not!

When we actually look closely at the loves and the losses we have experienced, most of us recognize that at times we have carried a heavy burden, but it was *our* burden. It is not one we would trade with someone else. Given the opportunity to exchange misfortunes we'd probably take our own burdens and depart.

Sometimes it seems we have chosen heartbreak but in reality we have chosen to care deeply for another. It's the depth of the love that makes the loss so unbearable. The love is our own, as the pain is our own. To trade one means you would agree to trade the other.

The emotional pain is a burden to be carried with gratitude and pride because symbolically it represents the love that was and still is a rich and rewarding portion of your life.

Coming to Grief

We came to grief,
as though it was
all that could be.
The dirt track twisted
and turned, but did
not fork.
There were no
crossroads,
no other towns to visit.
Only the one destination.

We came to grief,
it was waiting for us,
nowhere else to go.
We plodded down the hill,
entered the town and let
the gate shut behind us.

My hair is let down,
ashes are rubbed
on my face. I
turn to the wall
and endure.

© by Gillian Savage, Sydney, Australia
www.tirralirra.doc

BRAVERY

Being brave during the time of grief takes on new meaning. It's not the usual bravery that allows us to hide our feelings, but the type of courage that allows us the expression of our feelings. When we are brave, we won't allow our emotions to be hidden, to keep us from talking, to require us to "keep up a front."

Well-meaning people often say things that make us feel worse rather than better. For example, they encourage us to be brave—to substitute bravery for grief. If you delay the grieving process and put all your energy into looking brave, you will have to do the grieving at a later time.

First, you need to look after your own emotional needs. If you need to cry, that's what you should do. If you need to ask for help, or talk about the loss, you need to do that. The last thing to think about is how you look to others. "Keeping up a good front" blocks out the necessary grief-related responses and conditions.

An exaggerated sense of bravery may cause harm by delaying the process of grief, keeping you stuck in early days of grief. At first, you experience shock, disbelief, and extreme disorientation. Crying and talking helps you to move on to the next phase, which helps you to realize that the death is real. A show of bravery may make others feel less uncomfortable, but eventually you will have to move through the necessary phases of grief to find your own resolution.

Magazine publisher Michael Tynan MacCarthy talks about the death of his father, H. Neil MacCarthy, and how the months of reconciliation before his father's death helped him to face his grief. These excerpts were taken from *San Diego Writer's Monthly,* September 1992.

> Soon after I read Robert Bly's book, *Iron John,* Dad and I began trying to bond. We would write and call each other. He asked for a subscription of my magazine, *San Diego Writer's Monthly,* to show off to his friends.
>
> Dad's labored breathing into the phone told of his poor health. He admitted to a deteriorating lung condition, a legacy from his days as a production engineer in hazardous plants.
>
> Although now tethered to an oxygen tank, Dad would not curtail his routine. There was grocery shopping, biking, riding, and sailing on the Rappahannock, but most of all there was his writing. He was working on a new script for a children's play that he would once again direct and produce for the local library. Also, he was under contract to write a 1500-word column each week for the local newspaper while doubling as their proofreader.

I asked him for copies of old columns. Months passed. One day a big envelope containing a dozen of his vignettes arrived at the office. I showed them to the magazine's editor, and he thought one called *Father, There Is No Good-bye* would work well for *SDWM*. When I called Dad to ask permission to use the piece, there was a long silence. "You really want to use it?" he wheezed, his voice breaking.

When the June issue finally arrived, he called and said how happy he was we had downplayed that he was my father. He could now believe his piece had been accepted on its own merit.

A few days later, he and I began discussing the possibility of my traveling with him after the summer. His hope was that the two of us could drive up the East Coast so he could visit and reconnect with all his 11 children while he still had the strength.

Meanwhile, my editor and I were putting together the July issue, featuring poetry and essays about the male experience. Something told me I'd better publish the story about how I came to reconnect with my father in that issue.

On Fourth of July weekend, *SDWM* arrived special delivery in Virginia. Dad had a virus. In his weakened condition, fever raced unchecked through his now frail body. Still, he found the strength to read his oldest child's essay. Nodding, he smiled and closed his eyes. It was the last thing he read. Two hours later he died.

And so, dear Father, for you and me there is no good-bye either. Just a loving farewell and warm thanks to you for being my dad.

CHAPTER 3

CEREMONY

The ritual of a public funeral service, or memorial, seems to give an appropriate recognition to death. In considering the service, you might consider what the loved one would have wanted, but also consider what is comfortable for you. Ask yourself, "What ceremonies seem appropriate for the life of my loved one, and of our life together?"

Others may want to take part in the service, especially if your loved one was a member of a closely-knit family, a teen, or a younger child. Consider the wishes of others but do what's comfortable for you. It's gracious to be able to honor the grief of others but only if it seems appropriate.

Usually there is some public remembrance for your loved one, but you might also arrange for a private ceremony for your personal memorial. It can happen immediately or at a later time. A few close members of the family or a small group of friends can plan such a gathering with you, or you can have your own private remembrance. Some choose to create a ceremony on the anniversary of the death, or on the loved one's birthday. Others randomly select a place and time.

Ritual and ceremonies around death are created to help those who are left behind. Ceremony serves as a kind of protection in times of emotional stress, especially right after the death. Later, ask a good friend or a family member to visit the gravesite with you—or visit alone. Repeated rituals can continue to help you heal in the months and years that follow.

Michael A. Simpson writes in *The Facts of Death* (1979):

> Various acts of mourning have clear purposes. They openly acknowledge the reality of death and explain it once more in whatever way the current system of belief conceptualizes death. They allow for the open expression of grief, but in controlled and socially acceptable circumstances and forms, and they allow gestures of consolation and support from friends and relatives.
>
> For one final occasion, the dead person takes a central position in a social event, along with his or her bereaved relations. The rituals may honor the dead and define the shape they will take in our memories, or make preparations for the soul's journey or the life in another world. Rituals serve to provide a temporary structure at a time when the removal of an important part of your personal and social structure has left you adrift. They give you something to do when there's nothing to be done and you feel you must do something—without your having to search to be creative in devising something to do. Rituals can give you a set of familiar practices to turn to when the shape of life has become unfamiliar (p. 235).

In Stephanie Mendel's frequent visits to her husband's grave, she finds solace in the ritual of telling him what is happening in her life.

What We Tell Each Other

A large bird glides over the cemetery.
I have sunflowers for you, and read
you David and Holly's postcard from Egypt.
I tell you Doug rented a U-Haul, moved
even the windsurfer to his cabin. I ask
if you can come by to smell the tomatoes—
know I should have brought one with me.
I tell you the bamboo is coming up through
the cement in Mildred's garage. I thought
you'd be interested, but can tell you're impatient
and are waiting for me to simply lie down
next to you, so I do, and it feels good,
the way it always has.

© by Stephanie Mendel

CHANGE

The most immediate change we experience when a loved one dies is that they are gone. The one change we can't bring about is the return of our loved one. Things can't go back to "normal" or what they were before. We're likely to feel isolated. This isolation makes the world feel like a vastly confusing and chaotic place.

Consumed by the loss and our longing, we see the world and ourselves much differently from the way we did before. We think, "the world will never be the same." And in a very real sense this is true. Our world is permanently changed because we have lost a precious and vital piece of it. No wonder there's confusion and chaos.

Recognizing that we're in a terrible state of flux at this time will help us to be more patient with the confusion we are enduring. This is a time for faith that this confusion will surely pass and gradually diminish.

Usually, survivors are presented with a selection of alternatives. Like, should they sell the house? Move away? Make some changes in life style? Changes in their environment? Usually it's very difficult to make major changes when you're confused. So unless there is a financial crisis, there should be no moving, selling, or quitting.

If you're tempted to make any major decision, talk it over with a person you trust—preferably someone who has not been affected by the death. Remember you're not in the best state to make wise decisions and shouldn't get involved in a significant life change for at least a year.

The very nature of life is constant motion. It's important to realize that our life has changed because of this loss, but that our life was always fluid before this death occurred.

Carol Straudacher, in her book *A Time To Grieve* (1994), uses this analogy.

> Life is like the ocean. Even though we are stepping into the same ocean, we are not stepping into the same water. Like the water, the life we lived before the death has flowed on. The life that remains is also in motion and has been transformed by our loss. This will be time of change, a time to work toward readjustment and new understandings (p. 88).

Peggy and Andy

Death can make you see everything differently. Peggy lost her fiancé when she was 19 years old. Andy was killed in a tragic car accident. From that moment on, everything in her life changed!

Andy and Peggy were to be married, now she was alone. She was going to a college they both attended, now she attended alone. She was very close to Andy's mother and looked forward to joining the family. Now she could never do that. There would never be children with Andy as she had hoped. She was forced to view her life differently.

Grief changes your perspective, makes you rearrange your priorities. Often in the face of death our lives become more focused.

Grief became a teacher for Peggy. Couples that she and Andy had once been close to eventually drifted away from her; she had to change schools when the pain of familiar surroundings became too much for her; she grew closer to her immediate family; and eventually she began to date someone new. When Andy was gone, Peggy became more aware of her feelings, more aware of traits she had previously ignored in friends, and more determined to survive on her own.

It took a long time for Peggy to adjust to the changes in her life. At first, she clung to old friends and the familiar haunts of the college town. She was unable to move ahead as she hung onto what was behind her. Like a ship that is leaving port, she looked back trying not to lose sight of the shore. She failed to look ahead to discover new lands. There were several years of casting about, feeling adrift while she desperately tried not to lose sight of what had been familiar to her. Slowly time helped to change her direction and she had a clearer vision of a new life.

Change occurs only when we give up one life and enter another. Letting go doesn't mean no longer loving. It doesn't mean that we don't recall and care and yearn and cry! It simply means that our life now has an added dimension.

In time, Peggy found that the most wonderful parts of the life she lived with Andy were incorporated into her new life. After all, they had shared love, a need to get an education, the dream of marriage and family. She didn't simply lose a part of herself, but carried into the future a new part of herself that represented the bond she shared with Andy. She let go of one segment of her life to create and perpetuate another even while she was carrying forward the good from the past. Peggy took what she learned everywhere with her as she moved ahead.

CHOICES

Death made Peggy think more about the choices she had in life. It made her realize that she needed to be more open about her loving feelings. She wished she had told Andy how much she loved him. Although she said "I love you" on occasion, it was not said enough. She had rarely expressed her feelings openly. Now she chooses to communicate her feelings more freely.

Andy's death helped her change some of the aspects of her existence that displeased her. Peggy had been intolerant before Andy died; now she has become more tolerant of others. Sometimes she wavered about her education, but Andy's death made her determined to stick to previous goals.

A sudden death may provoke us to examine the things we wish to change and eventually make the choices that will create those changes. Our priorities may shift, time may seem more limited, our values may change. Therefore, our choices will be altered. Death shines a light on our life and that light may guide us in a different direction.

Sometimes death leaves you with a clearer understanding of permanence, as Martie Odell-Ingebretson indicates in the following poem written after the loss of her child, Michelle Lee Jameson.

You Leave Me With Permanence

Did you see that clear line
following the curve of the mountain
where the sky touched?

It whistled to me.
I could hear it 'round the house
as the leaves danced to get my attention.

And so I bundled my shoulders in flannel
and turned my heart to the north
and saw you there
dressed in those long stockings
and black leather shoes,
you were wearing the red velvet dress
even though I could have sworn that I covered it,
wrapped it tight with tissue
and snuggled it next to my wedding dress.

You must know how hard it is to touch,
because fabric lives and lives
while people die,
for you were wise even then,
and now that you know the answers
to all the questions that I have asked,
there you are
not a shadow, no,
but torched in bright beguile
galloping across the mountain
where your ashes feathered and fell
so many years ago.

I want you to know that you have taught me
about listening and patience,
you were never good at either then,
and as I watch you blow out
like a candle flame
you leave me with permanence.

© by Martie Odell-Ingebretsen

CONTINUING BONDS

When my husband, Bob, lost his older brother, Ned, this year, he knew he would continue to be influenced by Ned. He told me, "My mind seems to like to create intellectual drama. Ned used to see through my drama and remind me to keep it simple by checking the obvious first. I remember one incident when my car stalled and I was convinced the timing chain jumped a tooth. I proceeded to take the hood and part of the front end off, remove the radiator and expose the timing chain only to find it intact. When I called Ned, he said "Did you check the points?"

This was, of course, the most obvious cause of a stalled motor. The removal of two screws was all I needed to do. Almost everyday I reconnect with Ned when he steps into my intellectual drama and cuts to the chase and says, "Did you check the points?" Ned will be with me as long as I live.

Although words like "resolution" and "closure" are sometimes used to reference the grief process, many survivors know that there really is no definitive end to the relationship with the deceased. The loving bonds made in life continue beyond death. A grown child may continue to draw support from a dead parent, particularly if the parent was a source of strength, inspiration, and wisdom. At critical points in their life, this child may deeply sense the presence of that parent in a continuing bond.

So too, a wife may continue in relationship with her dead spouse when she makes decisions about her children, her life style, or her belongings. The life-plan set in motion through the marriage bond continues.

Even though these survivors know they continue in relationship with their loved ones, some grief therapists encourage them to break their ties with the deceased, give up their attachments, form a new identity, and reinvest in other relationships. Some counselors insist that "continued bonds" are unhealthy.

However, the newest trends in the grief therapy field point to an expanded view of bereavement. Dennis Klass, Phyllis R. Silverman, and

Steven L. Nickman, in their book *Continuing Bonds: New Understandings of Grief* (1996), claim the resolution of grief does *not* necessarily mean the mourner must disengage from the deceased. They claim the resolution of grief often involves continuing bonds that the survivor maintains with the deceased loved one.

In their book they describe various ways that survivors maintain continuing bonds with loved ones:

> **1. Renewal of Relationship**
> You may have a set of memories, feelings or behaviors that seem to rekindle the closeness you once had with your loved one. Memories can be the most precious gift we are left with and can become the most prominent, accessible links to the deceased. Anniversaries are a typical time for renewal of relationship.
>
> **2. Sensing the Presence of A Loved One**
> You may have times when you need to talk with your loved one. You sense their presence knowing that somehow they hear you. Then, amazingly an answer will come. In a time of crisis, you may find your strength has come from a source outside yourself. Upon reflection, you realize you were protected, watched over.
>
> **3. Incorporation of Ideas, Beliefs, and Values**
> Consciously or unconsciously, you may continue in relationship with your loved one by incorporating their ideas, beliefs, and values into your present life. In this way your relationship continues to be an integral part of your present reality, your new sense of self.
>
> **4. Creating A Symbolic Representation of The Deceased**
> You may stay in relationship with your loved one through a symbolic object or religious and social rituals. It might be objects of nature: a blue bird, a rainbow, the setting sun. It could be a work of art, music, or a special poem that brings your loved one back to you. It could be a religious service, or a family gathering.
>
> Every time you are brought back to remembrance, you continue the bond of relationship. The "coincidental" timing of sightings of your symbolic remembrance may have special meaning to you and deepen your ongoing relationship with your loved one (pp. 90-94).

Even though you may find references to the "resolution of grief" in other parts of this book, it's important to note that continued bonds with a loved one are not considered a lack of closure and therefore unhealthy or unrealistic. Today, more grief therapists are recognizing these connections and reexamining their old theory that the purpose of therapy is to sever all bonds with the deceased. Now they see that resolution of grief may include continuing bonds with the lost loved one.

Rosemary J. Gwaltney sees her lost child as an ever-present sweet phantom.

Sweet Phantom

Like a sweet phantom she haunts me still;

Giggling in my dreams; peeping through a crowd
Blue eyes sparkling, high voice calling me aloud.

Like a delicate fairy, her memories soar,
Time preserved tender her pixie lore.

Ever young, this dainty rider of my tears,
Snuggled in my soul through all these years.

Like a sweet phantom she haunts me still;

Perhaps she always will.

© by Rosemary J. Gwaltney
www.crossingrivers.com

COMMUNICATION

Death makes people feel uncomfortable because it reminds them that they will die some day. As people come face-to-face with their mortality, they're apt to seem uncomfortable in their communication with those who grieve. Some people engage in meaningless conversation that often sounds irrelevant or insincere.

It's confusing for the survivor to sort out what someone says and what they mean. Some people can't speak at all, but need to act out their condolences by cooking a casserole or baking a cake or sending flowers. These mixed social messages can be confusing.

Often it's necessary to seek supportive companionship among the friends and family who have survived a loss of their own. Sometimes it helps to reach out to another person who has recently lost a loved one. Showing kindness helps them and you. You can be thankful that such acts of kindness—both given and received—are possible in the midst of your loss.

When someone offers you advice or opinions that are not appropriate for your situation, it's best to be polite and hear them out. If, however, these remarks continue and become more hurtful than helpful, it might be wise to speak up, express your feelings and put an end to the conversation. Some people mean well as they try to help, but they have no direct experience with grief. Be patient.

YOUR COMPASSIONATE FRIEND

I can tell by that look friend, that you need to talk,
So come take my hand and let's go for a walk.
See, I'm not like the others—I won't shy away,
Because I want to hear what you've got to say.

Your child has died and you need to be heard,
But they don't want to hear a single word.
They tell you your child's "with God," so be strong.
They say all the "right" things that somehow seem wrong.

They're just hurting for you and trying to say,
They'd give anything to help take your pain away.
But they're struggling with feelings they can't understand
So forgive them for not offering a helping hand.

I'll walk in your shoes for more than a mile.
I'll wait while you cry and be glad if you smile.
I won't criticize you or judge you or scorn,
I'll just stay and listen 'til your night turns to morn.

Yes, the journey is hard and unbearably long,
And I know that you think that you're not quite that strong.
So just take my hand 'cause I've got time to spare,
And I know how it hurts, friend, for I have been there.

See, I owe a debt you can help me repay
For not long ago, I was helped the same way.
As I stumbled and fell thru a world so unreal,
So believe when I say that I know how you feel.

I don't look for praise or financial gain
And I'm sure not the kind who gets joy out of pain.
I'm just a strong shoulder who'll be here 'til the end—
I'll be your Compassionate Friend.

© by Steven L. Channing

This poem was written by Steven Channing after the loss of his 14-year-old daughter, Kimberly Susanne Channing—April 15, 1973–February 23, 1987. He is a former member of the Winnipeg Peer Counseling Service, Winnipeg, Canada. Steven started up several

Survivor's of Suicide Groups after his daughter's death. He credits the love, guidance, and understanding of the group in helping him through a difficult period. He says, "the more I reach out to others, the softer and firmer her memory comes back to me."

It's usually very beneficial to join an appropriate support group if you are struggling with grief. It's so much easier than trying to make it all alone.

CONDOLENCES

Unfortunately, some people come up with thoughtless and hurtful things to say when they mean to console us. People who lose children are sometimes told that they should be glad to have surviving children, or they might have more children if the lost child is their first born. These things are true but do not minimize the pain of this loss. Other children do not somehow magically make up for the loss and erase their special love and longing for that child.

Most inappropriate condolences—anecdotes, explanations, or advice—are usually generated out of a lack of experience with grief. People who have not lost a loved one often see grief as a temporary state that can be reasoned away. It's best to dismiss such condolences and concentrate on something that someone has said that is helpful.

Because no one can ever really know the weight of loss you carry, there's never a perfect condolence. Circumstances of death differ. Some survivors have time to prepare for death with the long-term illness of a parent; some parents lose a child to sickness or violence; some spouses lose the one person they depend on. Whatever the situation, there are universal characteristics that survivors feel after death—shock, anxiety, despair, confusion, disorientation, and longing. Condolences are generously offered to ease our pain. Often, the person has suffered a loss too, and has empathy as they remember the terrible burden they too carried. Most condolences are sincere.

Ted Reynolds expressed his condolences in this poem written for a friend lost before he really had a chance to know her well. Only through this poem could we understand that he too grieves.

Carol: Christmas, 1999

Her hands move through the thicket with care
Weeding and pruning the prickly hedges,
Restoring, against entropy, some semblance of order.
She offers me a running commentary.

One blossom is snipped because it doesn't measure up:
One to be displayed where its perfection can show;
One is taken that its neighbor may better bloom.

She warns me to use gloves when sorting out this tangle.
Not relishing the carving of thorns, I do protect my hands.

Before the year ends, she too is snipped.

I never learned to wear gloves on my heart.

CHAPTER 4

DENIAL

In *A Time To Grieve* (1994), Carol Staudacher says, "It takes a considerable time for our disbelief to dissolve. Until it does, we seem to be looking at everything through gauze curtains." We move and act but do not fully participate in our life. We can't. "The sounds and words around us that filter through to us do not seem to be the products of our own hearing. The rooms we move through are alien rooms and the world is a strange place with otherworldly features" (p. 14).

This denial is part of a protective mechanism within us that lets us deny the enormity of the death. We feel detached as we experience the disbelief at every turn. Only the smallest voice inside says: "The terrible thing that is happening to you is real. It isn't a mistake." Gaining clarity and a sense of reality may take months.

During the period when you are struggling with the reality of separation, you will need to do whatever you can to acknowledge the finality of the death. It takes a great deal of time to believe something you do not wish to believe.

If the death was sudden, your denial may be more intense, since you had no time to prepare for it. The news may seem so overwhelming that you cannot make any sense of it. Such intense responses may continue even after the initial shock.

It takes some time to think of your loved one in the past tense. We may make a mental note of something we want to tell them, or still say "we" and not "I." Such slips are normal and reflect the depth of the bond we shared. As time passes, these lapses will become less frequent.

ONE TULIP

It was Mother's Day. All week I dreaded this day. My sons had sent cards and gifts and telephoned, but Don, my husband, wasn't here. He died in April, a year ago, of cancer. That first Mother's Day went well, so much to do, but this Mother's Day was lonely and sad. My youngest son was coming home from college, but not until late afternoon. I decided to mow the yard.

When I was done, I looked out the back window and saw a flash of bright orange and red peeking out from behind a tree in the yard by the fence. I thought, That's strange. I just mowed and didn't notice anything. I never had any flowers in the backyard and neither did any of my neighbors. I walked out to the tree and there was one large red-orange fluted tulip with yellow accents, with the sweetest fragrance. I was so thrilled and immediately thought of Don. He didn't forget Mother's Day, because every Mother's Day he bought me flowers that we transplanted around the house. I plucked that beautiful tulip and brought it in the house and put it in a vase by the sink. It lasted four days—beautiful and fragrant. Each of those days I smiled and thanked Don for a wonderful Mother's Day.

Sometimes one tulip, or a simple musical lyric, can provide the therapy needed in the grieving process.

by Joan Jacobsen

DISORIENTATION

Many people say they feel cut off not only from others, but from themselves, from the whole universe, from God. R. D. Laing, in his book *The Voice of Experience,* explains it this way.

> The cut-off feeling is specific. It is not the same as being turned off. It is not the same as a sense of remoteness, or nostalgia, or pining for lost or absent love.
>
> When someone says he or she has to keep people at a distance, one knows that person is not cut off. The cut-off person need keep no distance. There is no possibility of intimacy, or dread of losing oneself in the other. There are no coils to be caught in. One is never more together than apart. All others are on the other side. No flow, or interchange, nothing, is felt to go on across the irremediable, irrevocable divide (pp. 132-133).

If the feeling of being cut off from the world persists beyond the early weeks of grief, it may be necessary to work with a therapist to help figure out what is the natural disorientation and fragmentation of grief and what is unnatural. Prolonged, severe fragmentation may indicate that the survivor has become stuck in the first phases of grief.

•

Some general disorientation is a natural part of the grief process, especially in the early days. Our world is so chaotic and confusing that it's hard to focus. Here's what you might do.

Each time you feel severely disoriented, you can take a few minutes to ground yourself. By using stress reduction techniques, you can help to remove those feelings of fragmentation. First, slow down, sit quietly, close your eyes, and try to clear your mind of all the thoughts that dominate it. Breathe in slowly and deeply, hold the breath for a moment, and breathe out very slowly, expelling the air in one long steady stream. Doing this breathing exercise just a few times should help calm your racing mind and bring focus to the sense of disorientation. This technique allows you to focus on slowing your body's rhythm to a normal rate. It grounds you. Do this exercise as many times as you need to relieve your feelings of being scattered and confused. Then, resume your activities.

DESPAIR

When we are first dealing with our loss, we see that nothing around us looks the same. Things we have seen all our lives take new shape, lose their color, or recede into the background. When everything looks out of control, we're looking at the world through the mask of despair, rather than the eyes of hope.

The people around us get out of focus when we grieve. It's as if they are disconnected, unimportant to us. Then when we begin to feel better our friends once again are our friends, our relatives come back into view, and coworkers seem real again. Despair takes you out of your world, hope brings you back to what is worthwhile around you.

In the following poem, Kirsti A. Dyer, MD, a medical doctor who has established a Web site called "Journey of Hearts: A Healing Place" (www.journeyofhearts.org), speaks of the initial darkness that envelopes all those who grieve, yet her poem ends in a message of hope as the darkness lifts to a new light.

DARKNESS

My light and my life
provided me hope for a future,
a reason to live
and the strength to exist.

Suddenly extinguished,
taken away without warning.
I was abandoned,

left in the darkness
trying to survive
searching for any glimmer
on the distant horizon.

I stand precariously
on a piece of solid ground
barely large enough for my feet.
Around me, a vast expanse
of desolation and emptiness
for as far as I can tell.

It waits
with extending arms
to engulf and surround me
in a permanent shadow.

I remain tenuously balanced
on this small bit of solid footing
Providing me the last vestiges of hope,
Unsure where to turn
or how to find an escape.

No path in sight,
it has decayed into the abyss.
No light to guide my footsteps,
it has been withdrawn.

In complete blackness
I close my eyes
waiting to fall.

A light appears before me
no, from within me.

I discover
a brilliance inside
An internal source of strength, power

and illumination.

This force surges through my body
filling me with courage.
I open my eyes once more in the darkness
finally lose my balance,
and descend
into the eternal night.

But in falling, I discover
that I possess wings.

With new courage, my own light,
and wings to save me
from the everlasting darkness

I take flight
high above the waiting chasm
towards a faint glimmer
far on the horizon
and hope.

© 1996 by Kirsti A. Dyer, MD, MS

The symbols of darkness and light Dr. Dyer uses in her poem are very real to those of us who grieve. We understand the dark despair that accompanies death. It tends to make all things seem black and insignificant. But we also know that after awhile, the color of things will brighten and return to their proper significance. With a renewed sense of hope everything comes into clearer focus. Things that once held great meaning to us will eventually regain their meaning. We will eventually take flight towards that new horizon of hope.

Sharon Swinney turned to poetry after losing her daughter. Her words in "The 'Spare' Room" describe the terrible heartache of losing a child, and the reality of shattered dreams.

The "Spare" Room

There's a room in our house, where the door is kept closed.
What lies behind it, nobody knows.
Perhaps I will tell you, if you have the time.

It has all sorts of things, you never know what you'll find.
There's a couple of prams, a cradle and a cot,
A rocking chair, a wardrobe and clothes, it's got the lot.
But if you open the door carefully, with ne'er a sound,
You may see my dreams, shattered on the ground.

For my hopes and dreams are there, more than a few,
Never to be realized, never to come true.

If you wait awhile, 'till the sun goes down,
You might hear them whispering and moving around.
Sometimes you may hear a cry,

But it's not real, it's just a lie.
They try to escape, in the cool evening air,
They slip under the door, they know I still care.
But it hurts so much when my dreams reach me,
The tears flow freely, why must it be?
I know when the sun starts to rise,
My dreams run back to the room and hide.
They cannot cope with the harsh light of day,
Only in darkness can they come my way.
Reality is painful, it hurts to the core,
But as the light starts to fade, I look to the door.
My dreams lie there, my shattered ones.
I hear them talking, soon they will come.

The second poem, "Reality Vs Imaginary," written a year later, captures the healing process. This poem, as the follow-up poem to "The 'Spare' Room," speaks of a way to get one's dreams to come out, face the light of day and the reality. Sharon writes: "I had to pass that room each time I went into my bedroom. It was so very hard to do. I knew that I had to face the room and everything it held for me, or I would never accept that part of my grief. I finally managed to go into Mary's room again. It was difficult, but I was glad I did. I was able to leave the door open after that."

Reality Vs Imaginary

That room is still there,
The one I call 'Spare.'

I feel it reaching out and calling me,
It is haunting me, and it's using my memory.
I have to go in. I have to go soon.
I have to face my memories, and dreams, in that room.

I'm scared to go in, it'll hurt too much,
My shattered dream, how deep it cuts.
I open the door and I go in.
The air is hot and stuffy, the pain begins.

My heart is heavy, I cannot breathe,
I remember her cry, I try to leave.
But I can't go, I must stay and face my pain,
Or all of this will be in vain.

I sit down and look around,
I put my Scotch (Dutch courage), on the ground.
I see her little night light, the memories flood in,
Of the tube feeds and medicines. Now my tears begin.

Those cold August nights, with the heater on high,
She was only in here a week, but how the time flies.
I feel a smile on my face, for the memories are sweet,
The haunting feeling is dulled. Will I try for defeat?

I see the highchair, where she will never sit,
But also the rocking chair and how she loved it.
The pain is softened, as my memories proceed,
My dreams mingle with them, I know I'll succeed.
I'm glad I went into that room which is 'Spare.'
The memories fill me with warmth, although my dreams
are still there.

I remember the cuddles, the love and the kisses,
Her strange little cry. Oh God, how I miss it.
Tonight I will sleep with the door open wide,
For my memories and dreams, are no longer to hide.

© 1995 by Sharon Swinney

DEPRESSION

For some survivors, grief does more than produce a general despair, it produces a deep depression. During this depression, life seems as if it's too much trouble. The smallest task seems insurmountable. Nothing interests you. You don't want to have to think or even be.

Depression and despair are common reactions to losses. These feelings may be especially acute if the survivor feels that God has let them down. Without God, we are alone. It's unrealistic and overly simplistic to think that the depression of grief is merely an expression of sadness.

There's a low point of depression where you may not find ordinary pleasurable activities enjoyable; you may become apathetic and slowed down, with no energy or motivation. In an intense depression, you may feel out of control, helpless, deprived, depersonalized, despairing, lonely, powerless, and vulnerable. You may feel that your life is meaningless and even that you yourself, are worthless. If you feel that even God has abandoned you, these thoughts only add to your sense of worthlessness.

It's a vicious cycle because if you berate yourself for your depressed state, you might make it worse by becoming inappropriately angry at yourself.

Most reactions to loss can be worked through. Some we talk about, or write about to find relief. But this is not so with a deeper depression.

Prolonged feelings of hopelessness cannot be ignored. When you suffer such feelings for an extended period of time, you may need to seek professional help. A qualified therapist can help you through the darkest times and suggest some special skills to cope with your feelings, or lack of them. Sometimes medication is necessary to pull you through.

Twenty-Five Suggestions When You Feel Depressed

1. Think of something you want that is available, then make a plan to get it.
2. Go for a long walk.
3. Think of people who bring you up; call one of them.
4. Listen to your favorite music.
5. Sing, chant, dance.
6. Take a shower or a long, warm bath.
7. Make a list of your strengths. Spend at least an hour concentrating fully on appreciating yourself.
8. Love a pet expressively.
9. Think of something you would enjoy doing for someone. Then do it.
10. Read a book on higher consciousness, love, or another enjoyable subject.
11. Forgive someone.
12. Consult a nutrition book and consider what you might add to your diet for pep and vitality.
13. Plan a trip that you think you would enjoy. Spend an hour imagining the trip and savor the exciting aspects of the experience.
14. Think about ways of relaxing. Choose one and do it.
15. Get a massage, or give yourself a body massage or a skin brush.
16. Begin something you've been putting off for a long time.
17. Consider ways to make yourself more enjoyable to live with.
18. Stop doing anything and just be for awhile.
19. Give something away.
20. Tell someone you love him or her.
21. Surprise someone!
22. Do breathing exercises for energy and calmness.
23. Clean up something. Organize part of your life.

24. Think of the most difficult person in your life. Concentrate at length, perhaps a day, on looking for ways in which he or she is actually good and admirable. Share these thoughts with that person.
25. Stare at the stars on a lovely evening and feel your oneness with the universe. Know the limitlessness of being.

Excerpt from Teen Age Grief, Inc., Newhall, California
(tag@thevine.net)

DISAPPOINTMENT IN OTHERS

Occasionally, a close friend will disappear from our lives right after the funeral is over. This could be the person we felt we could depend on and one of the persons we trusted to be there for us. When we realize we have been deserted, we feel angry and disappointed. We might feel this person has been selfish and superficial. Add this disappointment and loss to our aching heart and the pain seems unbearable.

There are times when it's necessary for us to forgive a friend for his or her avoidance of us. Perhaps they're dealing with their own feelings of inadequacy or confusion; perhaps they don't know what to do or say. Some people can be so frightened by death that they stay away—even those who you might expect to help you. They're not bad people. They may simply be people who, for whatever reason, are unable to join in our sorrow.

Some people are so afraid of their own feelings that they can be afraid of yours. Some people care, but they don't know where to begin. Some fear that if they begin to cry that they will lose complete control and become unable to stop. So they don't make a connection with you.

No one can understand the depths of your pain nor can you understand another's pain. Grief signifies the utmost in vulnerability, and you can't expect everyone to have the courage to come close to that vulnerability. Perhaps at a later time you will be able to discuss this situation with your friend. Give it time!

Please See Me Through My Tears

You asked, "How am I doing?"
As I told you, tears came to my eyes . . .
and you looked away and quickly began to talk again.
All the attention you had given me drained away.

"How am I doing?" . . . I do better when people listen,
though I may shed a tear or two.
This pain is indescribable.
If you've never known it you cannot fully understand.
Yet I need you.
When you look away,
When I'm ignored,
I am again alone with it
Your attention means more than you can ever know.
Really, tears are not a bad sign, you know!
They're nature's way of helping me to heal . . .
They relieve some of the stress of sadness.

I know you fear that asking how I'm doing brings me sadness
. . . but you're wrong.
The memory of my loved one's death will always be with me,
Only a thought away.
My tears make my pain more visible to you, but you did not
give me the pain . . . it was already there.

When I cry, could it be that you feel helpless, not knowing
what to do?
You are not helpless,
And you don't need to do a thing but be there.
When I feel your permission to allow my tears to flow,
you've helped me
You need not speak. Your silence as I cry is all I need.
Be patient . . . do not fear.

Listening with your heart to "how I am doing"
relieves the pain,
for when the tears can freely come and go, I feel lighter.
Talking to you releases what I've been wanting to say aloud,
clearing space
for a touch of joy in my life.

I'll cry for a minute or two . . .
and then I'll wipe my eyes,
and sometimes you'll even find I'm laughing later.

When I hold back the tears, my throat grows tight,
my chest aches, my stomach knots . . .
because I'm trying to protect you from my tears.
Then we both hurt . . . me, because my pain is held inside,
a shield against our closeness . . . and you,
because suddenly we're distant.

So please, take my hand and see me through my tears . . .
then we can be close again.

by Kelly Osmont

DISCOVERY

Grief is a Discovery Process

Some survivors try to think their way through grief. Thinking doesn't work. It's our hearts that ache when someone we love dies—our emotions that are the most affected. Certainly our minds recall, plan, and wish, but our hearts feel the pain. Grief is a healing process and we can't heal by our minds alone.

What are some of the things you discover? *First, you may discover a new perspective of your loved one.* When you go through the possessions of the one you love, you are forced to review their lives. Perhaps you will discover things you didn't know. The people, events, and things that had particular significance stand out. You may find answers to questions that puzzled you. Some realizations may be positive and some negative, but a clearer picture of your loved one will emerge.

In Memory of You

I find an old photograph
and see your smile.
As I feel your presence anew,
I am filled with warmth
and my heart remembers love.

I read an old card
sent many years ago
during a time of turmoil and confusion.
The soothing words written then
still caress my spirit
and bring me peace.

I remember who you used to be
the laughter we shared
and wonder what you have become.
Where are you now,
Where did you go,
When the body is left behind
and the spirit is released to fly?

Perhaps you are the morning bird
singing joyfully at sunrise,
or the butterfly that dances
so carelessly on the breeze
or the rainbow of colors
that brightens a stormy sky
or the fingers of afternoon mist
delicately reaching over the mountains
or the final few rays of the setting sun
lighting up the skies
edging the clouds with a magical glow.

I miss your being
but I feel your presence,
In whatever form you choose to take,
however you now choose to be.

Your spirit has become for me
a guardian angel on high
guiding, advising, and watching over me.

I remember you.
You are with me
and I am not afraid.

Secondly, you will discover things about yourself. The death of a loved one may provoke extensive, complicated self-examinations which provide an opportunity for self-understanding. It may prompt a further development of your compassion and the capacity to forge a stronger link to those around you. In that sense, the grieving period can be a rich discovery period because it takes you down to the depths of your own being.

Thirdly, your values may become clarified. As you survive the loss, you may rethink the way you've planned your life. Death makes you aware of time. You may reexamine your goals and your methods of reaching those goals. You may have more solid views about how you wish to spend the rest of your life. You may become willing to try new approaches and establish new boundaries for your behavior. You may become more willing to risk or you may see the need to draw back from the risks you are taking.

THOSE BLESSINGS I DIDN'T SEE . . .

Six weeks before this 1988 Thanksgiving Day weekend, my youngest brother, Jerry, jumped 500 feet to his death while living in Stuttgart, Germany. For most of my 50 years, Thanksgiving Day has meant a time for joy and celebration. This year, I hope you'll pardon me if I just feel thankful—thankful to be alive to recognize blessings I have, blessings I didn't see.

I am the eldest of 11 brothers and sisters. Jerry was chronologically the 10th child in our family. He turned 36 last July. Until six weeks ago, our family had never experienced death or tragedy within our ranks. Both my parents, although in their 70s, are alive and healthy. I recognized those blessings and thanked God for them, especially on Thanksgiving. However, there are two blessings I had been taking for granted. It took Jerry's violent plunge to wake me up.

When I went off to college with a scholarship and a smile, Jerry was five. My parents had been emotionally estranged for more than six years. Father lived in Maryland with a common-law wife and baby. My mother and siblings remained in a small Connecticut town to struggle through the brutality of abandonment. Jerry was small, frail, blond, and almost blind. He was also irretrievably lost for all time, but none of us knew.

Nobody understood in the '50s about emotional child abuse. Nobody knew how utterly worthless Jerry felt. None of us knew that his contrary behavior was a cry for help. The doctors called him a "sensitive" child, and so we made allowances for our youngest brother.

The next time I really noticed Jerry, he was a senior in high school. He had written me a special invitation to an original ballet composed at his school. He had only begun ballet classes as a senior, so I wasn't expecting much. I had raced by car to Connecticut from Washington, D.C. on a Friday afternoon and arrived just as the house lights went off.

The small New England town hall was packed. A hush fell over the audience as the curtain went up. In the middle of the stage was a life-size, Herculean-like statue with its back to the audience as little nymphs entered a palace courtyard and bounced and twirled to Mozart over the PA system. I didn't know what part Jerry was to play, so I settled into my seat ready to pick out my little brother whenever the male dancers came on stage.

Suddenly the muscular Greek statue began to move. It was Jerry. The ugly duckling had now become the beautiful swan. A graceful, powerful, leaping, spinning, and flowing swan. A Greek god swan. After the performance and his many curtain calls, I had to wait in line behind layers of adoring women, young and old, before I could finally give my "baby" brother a congratulatory hug.

A star was truly born that night. A star whose light of love and artistic excellence was to light our whole family for the next 18 years. What we didn't know was that his light was burning only on the outside. Inside, there was no Jerry. There hadn't been since his earliest days. His self-esteem had been flattened, crushed, and exterminated by the cruel emotional brutality into which he had been born.

And so as I try to make some sense of this 1988 Thanksgiving Day weekend, I thank God for the blessing of self-esteem—the feeling about myself that says that I am a worthy human being. A human whose worthiness is not dependent upon any other condition. I am, therefore, I am worthy. Whatever else may come to pass in the course of my life—success or failure, riches or poverty, fame or obscurity, sickness or health, family or alone—I am a worthwhile person. I didn't do anything to deserve or earn this blessing. I just have it. I've always had it. The trouble is I didn't bother to notice it.

How foolish to be so blind. To have a gift and not even know it. If I were rich or famous, surely I would spend much of each day giving thanks.

But the gift of self-esteem is more valuable because no one can take it from me. All the other gifts of this life including life itself can be taken away. But no person or circumstance can take the gift of self-esteem from me. Thank you, God.

Another blessing, which has gone overlooked in my life, is the ability to accept the love of others. I do not have to earn the right to be loved. I just am. It's a gift to me from others. I feel comfortable and empowered by their love. It's not a brag; it's simply a fact. There are some people in this world who love me, and I don't have to do anything special to qualify for their love—just be me.

Poor Jerry. He never understood that. Try as we may—his siblings, his parents, his ex-wife and lovers, his personal friends, most everyone who knew him—never heard us. He was unable to let our love flow through and over his entire being. He insisted that all love remain outside a certain special area that was his essence. He would not let love in there. He would taint it, he thought.

Thank you, God, for allowing me to know your love and the love of my fellow humans. Thank you for all my yesterdays, todays, and tomorrows. What a blessing is life itself. On this Thanksgiving Day weekend, I pray Jerry knows and understands what a blessing it was to be his brother. I miss him so.

by Mike MacCarthy

CHAPTER 5

EMOTIONS

It's painful to feel deeply. In fact a wide variety of strong feelings can disturb us by their intensity and power. Our emotions sometimes seem to be a curse. But the truth is, if you were devoid of unhappiness, despair, or longing, you might be devoid of pleasure and joy.

The great surges of emotion that come with death often seem overwhelming. It's as if such strong emotions will surely drown us. We wonder what we can do to escape such painful times.

We can remember that these strong emotions will pass in time. They are like the waves in the ocean, washing over us, removing from us some sorrow, despair, and longing. They keep coming until one day we find the feelings have weakened and no longer seem to be drowning us with their power. Each wave of emotion is actually healing you so don't fight it—let it do its cleansing work!

Our health will be adversely affected if we ignore our emotional needs. Our emotions are not disconnected from our physical body. They are part of the whole. We need to pay attention to our emotional care. This is especially true when we grieve because our physical condition may have already been weakened by grief. We can weaken it further when we ignore the expression of our emotions.

Once we unleash these emotions, their depth and intensity might surprise us. We might cry until we think we can cry no more—then start all over again.

It's like a deep well of feelings that resides inside us. We reach down into that well and pull until the feelings reach the surface; then, we reach down again. Eventually, the well becomes depleted as these feelings exhaust themselves. When we cry, we are dissipating the power of the sadness, despair, and longing.

It's very important to identify feelings because feelings can sometimes lead to certain ways of behaving. Feeling angry can influence our reactions to others; feeling hopeless can make us unwilling to risk. If we don't think before we act, we might later regret those actions. Some survivors have used the chart shown in Figure 1 as a record of feelings. (You can add to it if you find there are emotions not listed.)

By checking off the feeling and making a note of why you seem to feel that way on this particular day you may see patterns emerging. If you keep a record of your feelings for a given period of time, you will come to recognize and understand your patterns of feelings, and your actions, more clearly. Understanding your feelings doesn't heighten those feelings. It merely exposes "you" to yourself. When you see yourself more clearly and come to understand why and how you respond to things, including the loss of your loved one, then you are in a much better position to make important decisions. Zero in on *one* feeling on the list that seems to stand out. Ask yourself these questions.

1. What situation led to this feeling?
2. Do you understand why you feel this way? Explain why.
3. How did you handle the feeling?
4. Are you satisfied with the way you handled this feeling?
5. What changes would you make to better handle this feeling in the future?

If you learn to identify a feeling and the situation that leads to that feeling, you will soon be able to identify the situations that trigger certain feelings. Understanding your triggers can help you decide what situations to move toward and which ones to move away from.

afraid	disappointed	hopeless	overwhelmed
amused	foolish	ignored	sad
angry	guilty	incapable	trapped
anxious	happy	irritated	vulnerable
ashamed	helpless	lonely	worthless
bitter	hopeful	numb	yearning
detached			

Figure 1. The feelings chart.

Understanding your feelings can help you direct your feelings and not misdirect, or displace, them.

Displacement usually occurs when you're not conscious of doing it. For example, you might be hurt by an insensitive remark made by a fellow worker and go home and yell at the kids, even though you know the kids are just being kids and haven' t really been that bad.

Displacement happens when we try to push down a feeling or pretend it's not there. Unexpressed feelings often don't just disappear. Instead they get expressed in another way. Watching your feelings, or writing about them, is especially important during a time of loss. If you stay in touch with the feeling, expressing it to the proper person in a proper way rather than displacing it, you will retain some emotional control during this very difficult time.

ENDURANCE

When you feel you can't go on, when you feel no one could go on in such circumstances, you may remember that people often have more strength than they think they have. You can reach down inside yourself and tap into that reserve of strength that brought you this far. Remember moments when you persevered before. That strength was with you in the past, is still with you, and can take you the whole distance today.

As you struggle to keep yourself going to meet the challenges of having lost a loved one, you're sure to learn about yourself. As you persevere again and again, facing your grief head-on, you will learn about your endurance. A tragedy seems like it will kill you, but in truth it simply makes you stronger.

Stephanie Mendel's book of poetry, *March, before Spring,* chronicles the days leading to the death of her beloved husband. She demonstrates her sense of love and endurance in the following poems: "The Small Deaths" is the first, finding out about the cancer; "Your Last Birthday" tells of a final birthday; and "March before Spring" details the actual day of her loss.

The Small Deaths

The doctor tells you in a voice not shaking,
You have lung cancer and it's not fixable.
This is the most amazing thing
anyone has ever told us. We ask
a few questions. He answers,

Perhaps six months or less. He doesn't
know about pain. I don't say *thank you*
or even *bye* when we leave. We don't stop
for the new fuse for the rain gauge,
we get into bed and cry.

We tell ourselves we're lucky
it isn't a sudden death, like if
a plane went down. You say,
If I wear my new suspenders, I want
one side of my jacket to be open.

Afraid not many people
will come to the funeral,
you suggest door prizes.
I laugh like a teenager —
we're not old enough for this.

Later, I lay my hand on your rib cage,
bargain with the fist-sized cancer,
try to soothe it by telling it
if it grows slowly, it can live longer,
but I know it's too greedy to care.

Your Last Birthday

No more four-mile walks on the bike path,
then not even a stroll to breathe
the star jasmine in the front yard.
Too soon you couldn't walk downstairs,
or get to the chair beside the bed.

You slept more, ate less, scolded me
for force-feeding you like a goose,
said losing weight would make
the casket lighter, easier to carry.
I didn't think this was funny.

Doug made pasta for your birthday,
wore your chef's hat, your walking shoes.
I made a birthday cake, your mother's recipe.
Like a child, you asked if you could
have your cake before your salad—
but wanted no candles, made no wish.

I gave you yellow and white striped pajamas,
which you wore for visitors and sometimes for me.
You wanted to grow a beard. I asked death
to hold off until the gray stubble grew
to a generous shape.

March before Spring

When your heart stopped beating
my hand was resting on your chest.
While loss and courage struggled
to find a meeting place, I had to
phone hospice, the rabbi, wake the boys.
Were they *our sons* or *my sons* now?
Do I tell people *I love* you or *I loved* you?
Do I stop wearing my wedding ring?

Three times I closed your eyes,
three times they opened again.
This made sense to me, even in death.
David brought me a cup of orange spice tea,
Doug read you the letter he would read
at the cemetery. I hoped the hospice nurse
would lose her way, not come to write in
the time of death, call the mortuary.

Months ago, you had flung some
Of my bras onto the tall ficus
in the bedroom and hid the rest.
When I take out my black purse for
the funeral, I'll find them, and a jade ring
like the one that broke, and a note:
See if United can fly you up to visit me.

CHAPTER 6

FEAR

Nothing robs us of our ability to act and reason as effectively as fear. Fear goes hand in hand with vulnerability and death makes all of us feel vulnerable. Death takes our sense of certainty and turns it to uncertainty, our confidence and turns it to a lack of confidence, our strength and wisdom and reduces them to weakness and unclear thought. That's what happens when fear settles in!

Grief presents us with many reasons to be afraid. We face situations we could never have anticipated, and often deal with them alone. We have to meet these situations with a mind, body, and heart that is wounded.

Another source of fear may be the recognition that our usual coping patterns and problem-solving strategies cannot eliminate our grief. While they can help you cope with it, they cannot solve it as if it was a problem to be figured out and answered. For example, your usual approach to managing a difficult situation, such as identifying what needs to be done and then decisively proceeding immediately to resolve the entire matter, often will not work in the same way with grief.

You cannot control grief. Yet, you cannot avoid it either—many more problems will arise if you try to escape your grief. Therefore, the chaotic, unexpected, and intense experience of grief does not lend itself to the same logical and orderly processes of resolution, as do problems you typically may encounter. Consequently, it may be quite frightening for you when your usual techniques don't work.

This lack of control can make you feel more powerless and vulnerable. Additional secondary losses may be experienced since these coping and problem-solving strategies are less effective than usual.

Now the world seems unpredictable. You think you might die, too. Perhaps you're afraid to risk. Old phobias may emerge like being afraid to fly, or go on the subway, or even go into public places.

These reactions are a common response to the fear death engenders—but they are not a necessary response. We don't need to allow excessive fear to dictate what we do or think. Usually the way to deal with fear is to recognize the feelings that are linked to it. Write about those feelings.

If you're afraid to return to your job, write out your fears on paper. Think it through. What do you fear will happen? Will people around you make you cry? If so, what will be the consequences? How might you handle the situation? What situations do you fear the most? How can you avoid those situations or move into them slowly? Can someone at work help you? Fear dissipates when you confront it and think it through.

This fearful state is temporary and it occurs because our world has been shaken. Once we regain our strength, these fears will lose their power and we will be able to reason and act as we did before this loss.

For the first few months, there is no reason to force yourself to do something you don't really have to—taking a plane, subway or bus or even entering the house alone. But after you are further along in the grieving process, you may have to face the fear and actually engage in the dreaded activity. It may simply mean entering the house alone at night to prove to yourself that no harm will come of it. Each time you do this you put the fear behind you and gain strength. It's true that anything we dread can be faced and robbed of its power.

If you feel unable to enter your house alone the first couple of times, explain that fear to someone you trust and ask them to accompany you. Sometimes a simple prayer is the best antidote to fear. The 23rd Psalm is a popular prayer that often dispels fear.

> The Lord is my shepard,
>
> I shall not want.
> He maketh me to lie down in green pastures;
> He leadeth me beside still waters.
> He restoreth my soul:
> He leadeth me in the paths of righteousness
> For his name's sake.

Yea, though I walk through the valley
Of the shadow of death, I will fear no evil;
For thou art with me;
Thy rod and thy staff they comfort me.
Thou preparest a table before me
In the presence of mine enemies;
Thou annointest my head with oil;
My cup runneth over.

Surely goodness and mercy shall follow me
All the days of my life:
And I shall dwell in the house of the Lord
Forever.

Psalms 23:1-17

FAITH

Others have made this grief journey and have made it through. You can too! The times you have met with difficulties in the past and dealt with them can give you faith that you will be helped through this time.

For most people, in moments of deep sorrow it's difficult to believe that God, or any Higher Power, can help them. Doubts can creep in. They might ask, "How do we know if there's anything beyond this life?" No one knows for sure until we die ourselves. But if you look to the universe and examine its power and structure, it seems reasonable to believe there is order within the mystery. What happens beyond this life is part of that mystery.

Anything we do not know for sure demands our faith. Yet what is there within us as frail humans that believes we can possibly know all there is? We can never know and can only accept this mystery on our faith.

Be At Peace

Do not look forward in fear to the changes in life;
rather, look to them with full hope that as they arise,
God, whose very own you are,
will lead you safely through all things;
and when you cannot stand it,
God will carry you in His arms.

Do not fear what may happen tomorrow;
the same understanding Father who cares for
you today will take care of you then and every day.

He will either shield you from suffering
or will give you unfailing strength to bear it.

Be at peace,
and put aside all anxious thoughts and imaginations.

by St. Francis DeSales

FATIGUE

You are exhausted most of the time, if not all of the time. Grief creates exhaustion! Sometimes the simplest things seem to be overwhelming you. It's as if it takes tremendous energy to do the smallest thing.

When there is an energy-drain like this you may feel old and tired. Even young children who lose a parent feel old before their time. A person who loses a spouse will age. Just as physical illness makes us feel older, emotional distress takes its toll.

This is not a good time to neglect your physical well being. Living on coffee and snacks will not heal you, staying awake all night will weaken you. If you are hungry, eat; if you are tired, sleep. Let your body dictate what it needs.

There's nothing that says you need to accomplish "as much as you did before" during this grief period. In fact, this would be a good time to "stick to the essentials and take it easy." If you feel too tired to take a trip, reschedule it. If you can't attend a meeting, or go shopping, put it off until later. Protect yourself by slowing down! Use whatever energy you have to nurture yourself physically.

When my first husband died I was exhausted and felt that sense of numbness that is a part of early grief. Something inside of me kept saying, "Do only the basics—put yourself on survival mode." Each day I would decide what I needed to do to survive that day. And do only that much.

My emphasis had changed. Usually I looked at the day and thought how much can I accomplish this day. Then, I tried to do all the things on my list. Now in the shock of grief I gave myself permission to abandon the "accomplishment" thinking and find ways to simply survive. As time passed, I felt less fatigued and was able to do more.

The road beneath my feet

You are the road beneath my feet,
My path to who-knows-where.

Broad and secure in the bright sunlight,
You ease my way.
As a trail faint under the crescent moon,
You are my only hope.

You keep me safe in the wilderness
And show me the way forward.
Steadily, you encourage me onward,
Leading me surely to the light.

If I lose my way, I will look for you.
A single step brings me back.
My road, my path, my desire,
I will follow you faithfully.

You will be my guide and I will seek you.

At dawn, as I rise from my bed,
I will turn to you.

At noon, busy in my day,
My feet will not stray.

In the evening, tired from my efforts,
I will seek your comfort.

My road, may you be always beneath my feet.
Let me step lightly on you,
Let my eyes follow your line,
Let my mind know your direction.
My road, my path, my desire.

© by Gillian Savage, Sydney Australia
www.tirralirra.com

FORGIVENESS

Forgiveness is a gift to the one who forgives. It's a decision to enter a process of healing. It's a decision to let go of anger, resentment, ego, self-pity, shame, and personal hurt. It may take time but it's a gift to the self: one worth waiting for.

There are few survivors of lost loved ones who don't experience some shame about a specific thing they said or did when their loved one was alive. No one is perfect. We do things that we feel ashamed about. Making a choice to live in a state of shame can be hurtful to you; making the choice to forgive yourself is more positive. If feelings of shame persist, you might seek counsel by a professional.

Perhaps you harbor resentment about something done to you? It may have been a thoughtless act or even something hurtfully calculated. Then, after it was done there wasn't an apology and perhaps no discussion of it again. These thoughts can weigh heavily on us at this time.

Sometimes there's an unspoken kind of forgiveness that exists between loved ones. It would be nice if we could always make amends for wrongdoing. In a perfect world that would happen. But, most of us have some unfinished business in our relationships.

If there was some omission you regret, let it go. Start by forgiving yourself. Know that in all likelihood, your loved one forgave you. Know that your loved one was not perfect and did not expect perfection from you. Rather than punish yourself for an unresolved disagreement or some unfortunate act, you now need to trust in the goodness of your loved one and his or her capacity to forgive.

I remember a significant sermon I heard one Sunday. The topic—forgiveness. It was appropriate because I was struggling with my need to forgive someone close to me.

The minister made this statement: "*Forgiveness has already taken place in the heart and mind of God. It is only a matter of time until we catch up—in this world or the next.*" That statement changed my life.

The next week I spoke with the person who had wronged me, expressing my forgiveness and asking for his forgiveness. I explained that I was wrong to withhold my forgiveness because in the mind and heart of God forgiveness had already taken place. He began to cry. The bitterness ended there.

When you offer love and forgiveness, anger and resentment seem to melt away. A combative, unforgiving stance indicates that *you* have been harmed and usually is met with resistance. A loving non-aggressive stance can produce miraculous changes in a relationship. There's more power in peace and love than in a continued resentment. Forgiveness, whether it is yourself or someone else, brings you to peace and is a precious gift you can give to yourself.

Still and Always Love

Everything is so wild and spirited
today on the mountain where I left you
so long ago.

White gloves decorate the ridges,
cloaked and folded in soft slate clouds,
pines rise and red berries dot the hedges.

The river is cold and glinting with
the silver slither of life,
and on the ravaged tip of a tree
a crow sits watching
as slippery gilled and gasping
we give reverence to life.

The rocks along the road
are the color of the flecks of your eyes
and the mudded bank's dark pools open

and explode with the sound of riffles,
oh, how you loved the sound.

I think of you in frolic,
or spread in snow making angels now,
for always an invisible footprint
leaves its meaning along the path here.

Stay a moment,
as my heart feels February
like a hand print on this mountain.

I have found you
in June softened in yellow scotch broom
and in August cool and smooth
in the trunk of the manzanita.

The crow
with her knowing black eyes,
is that your head cocking,
your feather's ruffled,
waiting through this time of lasting?

Fly my little one,
be free from this need of mine
that roots you to a mountain,
for I will find you again,
when time melts into tomorrow,
I will find you still and always
in the middle of my love.

© by Martie Odell-Ingebretsen

FUTURE

When you are enmeshed in grief, you might see the days that are ahead as something to dread, a solid block of time that you're going to have to "get through." But time never comes in solid blocks. The future is a series of circumstances that come one day at a time.

Perhaps it might be better to see yourself not as a victim of time but as the architect of your future. Since the future only happens in one-day segments, ask yourself, "What can I do today to give me solace." It can be something as simple as stopping at the coffee shop for a mocha latte and a pastry. It could mean ordering a book at a bookstore, reading a book of meditations, or soaking in the bathtub at the end of the day.

Sometimes giving becomes receiving. When you try to help one other person with a gesture or smile, the day seems more worthwhile.

As you come to the other side of your grief, you will continue to find pleasure in small things. You'll be able to be enthusiastic about the things happening around you. In time there will be new sources of love and joy.

Death has a way of bringing life into focus by allowing us to identify our most precious assets. We learn the value of compassion, understanding, and kindness through the compassion, understanding, and kindness of others.

Material assets become less important. The true meaning of life becomes deeper for those who grieve as future decisions are made from a more humane heart. This was never more apparent than when Princess Diana was killed in 1997. People from all over the world paid personal and public tribute to her.

The worldwide response to Elton John's "Tribute to Princess Diana" quickly became evident. On October 21, *Candle in the Wind* was officially declared by the Guinness Book of Records to be the biggest-selling single record of all time. In only 37 days, the single reached 31.8 million sales. The words of this song helped the world ease their sense of despair at the death of a Princess and offered a final good-bye to England's Rose.

CHAPTER 7

GOOD-BYES

When someone we love dies, we don't say good-bye just once. We say it over and over. We live the good-bye. Because we set up so many rituals, daily bonds that we have shared, we have to distance ourselves from the expectations we had in our lives because of these bonds.

Especially during the first six months after your loss, you will need to say good-bye many times, in many ways. Perhaps you can talk to your loved one's photograph, make regular visits to the cemetery, or write a letter saying all the things you wish to say. If you have a support group, you can talk to the group about your difficulty letting go. There may be a special private ceremony in which you can release your loved one.

We all say good-bye in different ways, and in different places. For me, as a native of a coastal town in Maine, the ocean is my place of consolation. There are special places where I have had to go to say my good-byes.

For you, it might be a meadow, river, or the top of a mountain. Saying good-bye in these special ways, in these special places, helps us understand the reality of the loss. Amazingly, the reality of death can be apparent one moment and gone the next.

Closure means putting a final face onto something—a time of your life, a place left behind, or a relationship. Closure means finding a way to feel complete as you move on and leave that life, that place, that relationship.

Saying good-bye is a final gesture; however, you are not saying good-bye to your memories, your connection, or your ability to revisit your loved ones. You can keep the memory of your relationship alive in its own way. What you are doing is saying good-bye to those parts of the relationship that have ended and can be revisited only in memory.

There may still be questions unanswered and things that can't be said. Saying good-bye is difficult. When you are ready you might write a farewell letter like this:

A Good-bye Letter

Date:

To:

I will always remember ______________________________

Before you left, I wish ______________________________

Your death left me feeling ______________________________

I want you to know that ______________________________

(Finish the last part by saying anything you wish to say.)

After you finish you will probably want to reread your letter. From time to time you may return to this letter to reread it. Perhaps at a later time you might even add to it. Many survivors find the good-bye letter an instrument that helps them find closure.

GUILT/SHAME

If guilt sets in after your loss and if you begin to hear the words "if only I had" creep into your thoughts, it might be good to remember that most of us do the best we can at the time we are doing it. We have certain resources in that moment and are influenced in a completely different way at that time.

The things we may feel guilty about are usually without validity. It could simply be that feeling guilty is our way of making ourselves believe that we had some control over this death. The truth—we live in a vicarious world where tragic things happen. We are powerless over accidental death, violence, and fatal illness. By shifting the role of blame to ourselves, we may be trying to soften the recognition of our own powerlessness.

Then, there are those nagging petty regrets. Like having been too critical or having complained too much or just having spoken up too much. You're not perfect; and no relationship is perfect. Try to remember the loving moments not the negative ones. If your relationship was never as positive as it could have been, remember that it takes two people to interact. Perhaps your loved one suffered from his/her own difficulties and wasn't ready to, or capable of, a more loving relationship. It makes no sense to rehash the past and live in a state of constant guilt.

In *Guilt is the Teacher, Love is the Lesson,* Joan Borysenko, Ph.D. (1990) wrote:

> Whereas healthy guilt opens the way to increasing self awareness, resolving our difficulties, improving our relationships, and growing spiritually, unhealthy guilt keeps us stuck in a continual restatement of our presumed unworthiness—a state of constant shame (p. 27).

Let guilt serve you in a new way. Let it be productive by teaching you how to react in other relationships. Perhaps it will prompt you to make amends to another loved one, or to open up new avenues of communication with someone, or to strengthen existing bonds of love. Let guilt serve you rather than defeat you.

GROWTH

As you examine your relationship with your lost loved one, you may find yourself growing as a person. At first you ask, "How will I go forward? How can I emerge from this sadness so that I can function in the world?" It helps to know you're growing.

Each day take the time to list the things you need to do. In the first few weeks it may be very simple. Eat something. Take a bath. Call a friend. Then as time goes on you will do more and grow to a new place.

Probably you won't see your own growth at this time. Others may have to tell you what they see. Here is where a support group can help. Everyone there has gone through a similar experience and can recognize your signs of growth. They can remind you of how far you have come.

If you can, keep a journal. In it you can incorporate your observations, record perceptions, and identify strengths and weaknesses. Then, you can reread your journal from time to time just to chart your growth. If you can't journal and can do no more than keep a list, that's fine. Keep the lists. As the days go by, reread the earlier list. You will see how you are growing; how you are coming back to life. By writing, you can help clarify this process of self-discovery, this journey that is your life.

Life is a Journey

Birth is a beginning
and death a destination
And life is a journey:
From childhood to maturity
and youth to age;
From innocence to awareness
and ignorance to knowing;
From foolishness to desecration
and then perhaps to wisdom.
From weakness to strength or
from strength to weakness
and often back again;
From health to sickness
and we pray to health again.
From offense to forgiveness
from loneliness to love
from joy to gratitude
from pain to compassion
from grief to understanding
from fear to faith.
From defeat to defeat to defeat
until looking backwards or ahead
We see that victory lies not
at some high point along the way
but in having made the journey
step by step
a sacred pilgrimage.

Birth is a beginning
and death a destination
And life is a journey;
A sacred journey to life everlasting.

Author Unknown

GRATITUDE

You might wonder how you could think one grateful thought at a time like this. You have lost a loved one and everything seems bleak. You might even find it difficult to see the good in life itself. You may not even value your own life these days.

Gratitude is the key to finding your way out of your grief!

In the November 2000 issue of Oprah's magazine, "O," Marianne Williamson says,

> Very often I say, "Thank you, God" when a gift in my life is packed in silk and satin and wrapped in ribbons and bows. But just as often, I say thank you when the gift has been wrapped in heartache. Thank you, because I'm determined to learn the lesson. Thank you, because I know there's a gift here, even if I cannot yet see it (p. 119).

Think of the things you have to be grateful for. It may start with small things: the gesture of a friend, the reappearance of old friends in your life, children, grandchildren, the beauty of flowers, the sound of a hymn. It can be more complex things like the ability to remember, to pray, to know God, and to have loved. It can be as simple as the next breath you take. There are always things to be grateful for, even in the darkest hour of your life. Make a gratitude list today.

____

____

____

____

____

Never fault yourself for the depth and strength of your grief. It usually reflects the depth and strength of your attachment to your loved one. Reflect on that love and be grateful for it.

It takes a long time to come to terms with the new status we face after a death. Only gradually can we identify things to be grateful for; only in time can we take an inventory of the good we have taken from that relationship. In the future, you may appreciate what you shared rather than what you missed. Gratitude is the key to that appreciation.

And if it was a troublesome relationship? Even if the only thing you learned from a difficult relationship was that you do not want to repeat that kind of relationship, you have something to be thankful for.

In time you will be able to see that life brings lessons and gifts. And not all lessons and gifts are packed in silk and satin and wrapped in ribbons and bows. Many gifts are wrapped in heartache and come from our darkest moments of despair. These are the spiritual victories.

GOD

Sometimes in times of great loss, we wonder why God allowed this loss to happen to us. We are disappointed that God didn't protect us from this pain. Yet deep inside we know that no one is exempt from loss. Everyone must die. We will die someday.

Grief brings us face-to-face with our own mortality. We think of what will happen to us when we die. Many questions may surface about a higher power, about the possibility of the immortality of the soul.

For many years, I believed God was a punishing God. If I were bad, bad things would happen. If I were good, then, of course, good things would happen to me. God would see to that.

As life seasoned me with disappointments and loss of loved ones no matter what I was, good or bad, I learned to view God in a different way. I no longer made God responsible when bad things happened to good people. I came to understand that God is Love and that God's will for me is joy. It became inconceivable to connect life's pain to a loving God.

You might ask, "What if I lost a child in a tragic accident?" What would I say then? Tragic accidents happen in the material world, love endures in the spiritual world. In my mind, God loves me and that does not change.

Sometimes in the throes of grief we feel like God has abandoned us. In truth we may be blaming God and find it hard to pray, hard to draw close to God for support. At a time when we most need acceptance of God's love, we retreat into anger, hurt feelings, and fear.

After the death of her third child, Mary Beth, Sharon Swinney wrote this poem because people told her it was God's will that her child died. "I became angry at people telling me that the God I believed in since I was a child had meant this to happen. I can't accept that. But I can accept that things happen for no reason and that God cries at the injustices in this world."

My God or Your God?

"It's God's will,
And it was meant to be."
This is what some people,
Say to me.
Do they really believe this,
Of our father above,
That He can be so cruel,
When he himself is Love?

Think about it people,
Think about what you say.
My God loves me,
He would never hurt me this way.
He did not plan it,
It is not his will.
It's because we are human, That we fall ill.

You need to justify things,
Find a reason why bad things happen.
So you credit your God,
You say this is his retaliation.
But my God is kind and caring,
Suffering was not part of His plan.
You say your God planned it,
Does he enjoy the pain of man?

My God is a loving God,
A father to us all.
He did not want our life to be like this,
Mankind did cause the fall.
Can you accept that things just happen,
With no ryhme, nor reason, or plan?
Cause I've got a question for you,
Answer it, if you can.
Your God and my God,
Only one does exist.
Which one would you choose,
For your eternal bliss?

© by Sharon Swinney

Everyone comes to his/her own faith in a higher being by taking their own spiritual path. Everyone develops his/her own personal relationship with the God of their understanding. If you find yourself full of questions at this time discuss these concerns with someone qualified to give you guidance and help. A spiritual advisor, perhaps. There is always more to learn about God and the mysteries of our relationship with God.

CHAPTER 8

HUMANNESS

Sometimes we come to a more spiritual place when forced to recognize our own human frailty. Death reminds us of that frailty. When our parents die, we may recognize that our bodies also will age, become diseased, and we will die one day.

When a loved one is murdered, we recognize how one person's violence can destroy human life. We are reminded we are not immortal; our life can be snuffed out in a moment.

Reminders of our humanness can lead us to a place of humility. Perhaps we're not exempt from the vagaries of life; perhaps the material body is not the only thing there is; perhaps there's a spiritual side to consider.

Death can bring the one who grieves to a place where they look into their soul for peace and solace; to a place where they need to reach out to God for support; to a place where they accept the limits of their humanness and appreciate their lives at a new spiritual level.

Death has always taught me these lessons. It has said to me, "Look at your life. It's transitory." "How are you living this transitory life?" "If you were to die tomorrow, what would you do today?" Death teaches us lessons about our humanness. We may begin to see the spiritual side of our existence as it runs parallel to our everyday life. Susan Dane, in her poem "Parallel," asks us to think of the possibility of another spiritual world that co-exists with our everyday material world.

PARALLEL

The dead are never really dead.
Their world runs parallel,
half here, half not,
a double exposure.
We box up life for our convenience,
but they come and go
on some indiscernible whim,
lean over our shoulders,
interject in conversations,
and visit their old haunts, nostalgic.
When my niece was barely three,
she saw my father in the bordering marshes,
wearing his hip high boots,
feeding the widowed swan.
Dad looked up and waved.
Katie waved back excitedly.
We told her she was wrong.
It was impossible.
But that evening we stood by the window
a long time watching.

Definition makes our world so safe,
keeps it all in place;
But when we sleep, I suspect
we too break with convention,
trespass protocol and time zones
to wander about in the nebulous parallel.
Perhaps to them we seem transparent,
thin, half there, half not.
In the morning we say it was a dream,
we've been somewhere;
the places and names we can't recall,
but on the tip of our mind, something,
something ever so near, everywhere,
and gone.

HURT FEELINGS

Anger is a natural part of grief. In most cases we tie anger into hurt feelings. We feel angry because a friend didn't reach out to us when we really needed them. We feel hurt when people who were close before now begin to shy away.

Hurt feelings come up frequently when widows and widowers are treated differently by friends because they are no longer part of a couple. It happens when parents who have lost a child see that they are making other parents uncomfortable. There are social implications to death situations: these changes can cause misunderstanding and hurt feelings.

A person who grieves also has to acknowledge that some people can't face their own humanness. They become terrified in situations of death and grief. To the one who grieves this seems callous because, after all, they have suffered the greater loss.

But the truth is we will have friends who are incapable of offering the support needed. Some perhaps can't even attend the funeral. It doesn't mean they don't care, it simply means they can't cope with such an emotionally demanding situation.

At this time it's not wise to expend too much energy at being angry or hurt by someone who is unable to help you. Rather, turn to those who can and focus your energy there.

TURN TO ME

When you look out the window,
you will see me.
When you stir your tea,
you will taste me.

You will find me in the papers on your desk
and the softness of your eyes.
You will find me in the ringing of the phone
and in the arch of your back.

You will reach for a pencil
and touch me;
You will pick up a folder
and there I am.

I am love and I am here,
turn to me, let me in.

HOPE

Where do you find the hope to continue? There are so many times when you feel like giving up. So how do you get beyond the despair? The answers lie in the very fact that you are experiencing your grief—not walking away from it or pretending it isn't there. That's one of the major reasons to have hope.

Hope stays alive when we accept the possibility of change. And, all things do change. Periods of sadness and despair are not endless. They too will change. How they change will be up to us!

It's wise to remember that "If nothing changes, nothing changes." When you feel yourself slipping into a place that seems hopeless, reach out of that sadness and despair to move toward change. You can prod yourself forward by moving in small steps toward change.

Call a friend. Go for a walk. Talk to a neighbor or a stranger. Help another person in some small way. If you assign yourself one task of reaching out each day, in time, things will change.

It's by involvement with other people that we keep ourselves engaged in life—and life itself is hope. Choosing life means, "I continue to move ahead this day. I choose to live!" As you move toward life, or hope, you will notice the burden of sorrow lessens each day. Mothers of young children who lose a husband often say that their children kept them going.

I know this to be true. When I was fourteen years old, my father died leaving my mother with eight children ranging from two to fifteen years old. The depth of my mother's loss was overwhelming. It hung like a mantle over every nook and cranny of our house.

There were days when you could feel her sorrow in the kitchen, the bedroom, and the living room where my father's favorite chair remained empty. My mother's sorrow lived in our house but she chose to go on with her children. She cooked our meals and fed us, washed the clothes, got us off to school, and survived one day at a time. As difficult as it was for her, she chose to move on with a hopeful heart. In doing so, she taught us to live on with hope.

I remember my mother's fortitude in this way:

MOTHER MAINE

The gray shingles of the cottage were weathered,
like the torn towel, hung with frayed edges
flapping there, held up by two gray pins.

The woman's hands were wrinkled,
white from the bleach in the pot where she
boiled the towels.

Her hair was coarse and wily—
it fought with the wind—
as she took the pins from her pocket
and pressed them into the line,
edges overlapping.

Out in the harbor, a sailboat struggled
with wash-board waves, its energetic
crew placing hand over hand on taut line,
nearly yawing, filling sails, now letting them go.

"A magnificent day for sailing in York Harbor,"
they said. But she didn't seem to notice—
That view, this summer day, lost in grief,
It was all she could do "to hang the wash."

© by Christine A. Adams

HEALING

When we suffer any blow, we need to heal. Although we may think of grief as a negative thing because it causes confusing powerful feelings, and even anxiety, in reality it's a healing force.

Fearing to grieve can hold back the healing. After a loss we need to acknowledge the deep powerful emotions that strike us knowing they will not harm us. We won't be damaged or fall apart. Actually, the way back to a kind of normal existence is the "way through."

Talk when you need to talk, take action when you need to and contribute to your own recovery. If a trusted friend or loved one is not always available, your journal can become a trusted friend, a place to keep thoughts and feelings, a place to find new awareness. It's one of the best therapeutic tools.

Just find a notebook that is the right size and design for you. Reveal your inner self in the pages of this book. Say those things you may not dare to say aloud. Allow yourself complete freedom and then lock the journal away in a safe place.

William Shakespeare said, "What wound did ever heal but by degrees." So it is after death, healing involves progress. When we hurt ourselves physically, we don't expect the cut to heal immediately. There are degrees of healing within the process itself.

Just as the body produces new cells to replace the damaged cells and skin heals over a wound, so it is with grief. Bit by bit mind and soul are being repaired. Most of the time healing is slow and invisible. We become impatient and think we aren't making progress. But we are!

As you review and express your reaction to the death—talk to others, join a support group, or write in your journal—your mind and heart becomes accustomed to the loss. Keep going! You are healing.

What about setbacks? What about those moments when a deep grief returns just as we think we're moving ahead? Although setbacks are confusing, they're perfectly normal within the healing process. Usually we go ahead for a long time, then get set back, then move ahead again to a new place of healing and awareness. Rarely does anything move forward without complications or setbacks—some highs and some lows. The grief process is the same in its progression.

Although it's difficult to do, we need to understand and be patient when we slip back. There's no use in denying the emotion—just acknowledge it as part of the process. Slow down when you slip back into your grief. Take care of yourself at this time. Remember that even though you will slip back from time to time, these recurrences should get further and further apart in time.

Joy and pain live within your heart. If you deny the pain it may persist. Acknowledge it as you acknowledge your joy. There's no such thing as "being over this." The heart never forgets. It seems there will always be some uncried tears.

At first, you may cry every day. Then, gradually days will go by without tears. It doesn't mean you have forgotten your loved one or never loved them. We don't grieve longer because we love more. There's no timetable. When the tears seem to be gone, it simply means you have worked your way through the initial stages of the healing process. Love never dies.

Simply cry until you no longer need to cry, allowing the healing to happen at its own pace. Know that your love can't be changed by outside forces, it remains strong within you. Ask yourself "are you getting the care you need?"

THE CARE YOU NEED

Are you getting the care you need?
—the time to sit by the window
watching the birds in the feeder;
—the quiet to read a little Leunig?

The care that puts a mug
of tea at your elbow,
refraining from anxious reassurance.
That allows silence
to nourish the air,
making routine a hallowed place.

This care frees you from decision,
If you're tired, you must rest.
Restless? Let's walk.
Lifted of all burdens, you
take your allotted place
at the sink—washing or drying
as requested.

Let the rain wet you,
Let the sun dry you,
Let quiet care enfold you.
Lay down your load,
your strength is not needed now.
Lie in the shade, it is siesta time.
The journey will wait.

No sentiment riffles the calm,
neither approval nor disapproval.
Quiet acceptance pervades
the fabric of the day.

CHAPTER 9

I

IMMOBILITY

It's natural to become inactive and withdrawn after a death. Somehow you may feel as if you're standing still while the rest of the world goes on as usual.

I remember returning to the classroom after my mother died. It had only been three days and I was still in shock. The lesson I was teaching was Geoffrey Chaucer's *Canterbury Tales* (1400).

As I put the pictures of the various "pilgrims" from the poem up on the screen, my students would read the descriptions by Chaucer. I felt as if someone else was directing the lesson. It was like I was the observer in my own classroom. If I had not taught Chaucer so many times before, I could never have taught it on this day. My mind and body seemed frozen in some kind of pantomimed lesson. I just got through each day any way I could, drawing on the resources of experience and previous knowledge.

Whether we participate in life or not, it will go on. My students needed to move ahead in their lessons so they could finish the unit on the Middle Ages. That was the reality of the situation. If I had stayed home for more than the three allotted funeral leave days, someone else would have had to teach that lesson. They probably would not have the preparation and experience to explain it fully and my students would lose out. Knowing that, I returned to school, knowing that I moved on, even when I wasn't emotionally ready to teach that class.

When we can't function, there's a natural tendency to blame ourselves for any disharmony, confusion, or mistakes that happen in our absence. Our sense of duty and guilt can push us on. Sometimes it's good to be thrown back into the routine and let the healing begin but it's never easy in those early days.

Finding a balance between the natural desire to retreat after a death and our need to avoid the difficulties that will present themselves if we retreat is part of the work of the grieving process.

When I returned to the classroom that week, I did only what was essential and eliminated anything extra. I didn't attend the faculty meeting after school, or offer to meet with students after school. Slowly, I worked these things back into my schedule. It's not realistic to think you're responsible for everything and everyone around you—retreat from some of the responsibility until the sense of immobility lessens.

Emily Dickinson has captured the surreal feelings that take over our minds in those early days:

I Felt A Funeral in My Brain

I felt a funeral in my brain,
And mourners, to and fro,
Kept treading, treading, till it seemed
That sense was breaking through.

And when they all were seated,
A service like a drum
Kept beating, beating, till I thought
My mind was going numb.

And then I heard them lift a box,
And creak across my soul
With those same boots of lead, again.
Then space began to toll

As all the heavens were a bell,
And Being but an ear,
And I and silence some strange race,
Wrecked, solitary, here.

by Emily Dickinson

ISOLATION

In these first days of grief, we're apt to feel immobilized, as we seem to float through the activities of the day. We go from one necessary task to another; we see one person and another with no seeming connection to what is happening. It's as if we are in the world but isolated within the depth of our own feelings.

It's no wonder that we might wish to isolate ourselves from the world whenever possible. A certain amount of isolation is beneficial. But sometimes a survivor will isolate when they need to talk simply because they don't know where to begin; or they're afraid to show their feelings. Children and siblings are vulnerable because they may wish to be with those who openly mourn but don't know how to join them.

Isolation can have personal benefits but not if the isolation is constant and continuous. We can help those who survive by recognizing the hazards of retreating into a totally private world. Usually, everyone benefits from talking about their feelings. It's hard to help someone else when you're grieving yourself. Yet all those who grieve, quite likely, share thoughts and needs in common.

When my child, Timothy, died a few days after he was born, I felt trapped in the hospital ward healing from a pregnancy that left me swollen and sore and childless. The minutes seemed like hours. The drab colors on the walls reminded me of the agony of my situation; the sight and smell of flowers reminded me of the funeral service we would arrange; the sound of the intercom screamed at me. The joy of mothers and fathers as they welcomed their babies into the world was more than I could bear. I couldn't stop crying amidst such joy. There was no escape. But I couldn't stay trapped in my room.

When I heard that another woman had lost her twins, I sought her out. She had lost both children and had no children at home. At least I had my first born son. My heart went out to her. We talked endlessly just trying to make it through. Without her I could never have survived the pain of that hospital ward. Being near her made me grateful.

One of the poets used extensively in this book is Rosemary J. Gwaltney, a remarkable woman who, with her husband Dale W., has dedicated her life to the adoption of some healthy children and some terminally ill children.

On her Web site, www.crossingrivers.com, she wrote this:

> It was our choice, in love, to build our family through adoption. Many of our children were healthy. But some were dying, or expected to die, from one cause or another. These were precious children whom others were too afraid to love; who needed a family perhaps more than any. Through a full three decades of parenting, one child after another, we have loved. The bonds of our love for each other grew extraordinarily deep, child by child. The griefs of earthly partings have been overwhelming; and only God's love and promises of Heaven have carried us all through. For we have not lost forever. We have laid up treasures in Heaven.

In poetry, Rosemary remembers her children:

On Visiting My Baby's Grave

No words to say; no words to say;
I visited her little grave today.

~ ~ ~

A stone in the grass so square and dry,
Whispers her name to a frigid sky.

~ ~ ~

My heart's desire lies still, lies deep,
So dear and small in a dreamless sleep.

~ ~ ~

I come away; I come away;
Chilled and alone with no words to say.

www.crossingrivers.com

Bronzed Baby Shoes

Bronzed baby shoes
giving me the blues,
bring with a tear my yesteryear;
her dear emphatic twos.
Who knew how much we'd lose?

~ ~ ~

Tones of gold in browns, and shaded,
sing to me how life's been jaded;
coming undone; reflections run;
epoch sweet by loss invaded.
Our realm now compressed and faded.

~ ~ ~

Daughter of mine;
love so rich and fine
still haunting me from memory,
time after lonely time.
Chanting in somber rhyme.

www.crossingrivers.com

IDENTITY CONFUSION

The altered sense of self that people experience after they lose someone integral to themselves and their lives creates an identity confusion. This confusion develops from the sense of physically, as well as emotionally, losing a part of yourself that makes up your identity.

This confusion comes not only from the sense of separation you feel from the person to whom you were so closely connected, but also from your own awareness of the loss of parts of your identity that had been validated by your relationship with your loved one.

For example, if you lose your life's companion through the death of your wife, you also lose that part of yourself that played the role of husband opposite your wife. This role irretrievably has been taken away. Even if you should remarry, that part of you that existed in the special and unique relationship you had with your first wife is no more.

In this sense, part of your "self" dies along with your loved one. This makes some of your grief for yourself, as well as for your lost loved one. Losing this part of the self can make any survivor confused about who he/she is anymore. This confusion can last until such time as the processes of mourning have helped you to establish a new identity.

By recognizing these underlying causes of anxiety that are part of every grief process, you can defuse their power. By sharing fears about your identity with a trusted friend, you can keep this fear from escalating while you grieve. Friends can help us by simply assuring us that it's normal to be confused about who you are. It's normal to be fearful and anxious at this time.

Activities—your environment, your schedule, your circumstances—have changed because you're no longer Mike's mother, Bob's wife, or Betty's daughter. Not only do activities change, your emotional make-up changes too. You had an emotional place for the role you played. You were proud of Mike's achievements, you enjoyed the respect you received as Bob's wife, and you felt comforted in your relationship with your mother.

In May Sarton's *Shadow of A Man* (1950), the main character, Frances Chaubrier, has just experienced the death of his mother.

> He was here on the steps of his mother's house, Francis Adams Chaubrier, and yet he asked himself, "Do I exist?" For the last few hours it had seemed as if his very existence were suspended. There was no simple answer to his philosophical question, even as he asked it, he proved his existence as a physical being, by walking quickly down the hill, listening to his own footsteps as if they were somehow reassuring (p. 14).

All those who grieve must assure themselves that they exist but not in the same identity as before the loss. Death has revised our identity so it is necessary for us to reestablish for ourselves who we are, what we want, and what our methods are to achieve new goals.

INNER PEACE

Those survivors who run away from grief may never achieve inner peace. It's through acceptance that we come to serenity. For most of us this place of acceptance doesn't come easily. We walk a long hard road before reaching this new place of tranquility.

Adolescents who lose a teen friend in some tragic way sometimes find it hard to accept the loss. Perhaps it's because the death of someone so young seems out of context with nature. In my work with high school students, I have found that many teens are able to rebound, come to grips with their grief and move on. Yet, on occasion, I have witnessed some who seemed frozen in their grief, staying in the initial phases of grief for a long time.

In my school, a popular senior was killed over the summer and a group of his teammates, unable to accept the death, immortalized him by meeting at his gravesite every weekend for months. There they drank until drunk and commiserated in their loss.

It wasn't until one Friday night when they returned to the school and spray painted the building with an obscenity that expressed their frustration that the school and community realized how desperate they were. They were still very conflicted and were crying out for help. Luckily, the school officials made sure they got professional help. In time, they were able to face the loss and go on.

The death of someone we love is not something we "get over." We walk through our grief, giving ourselves time to feel the sorrow. Then, we begin to view our lives from a changed perspective coming at last to accept what has happened to us. This acceptance is the gift at the end of the long road of grief—a gift we can give to ourselves by sticking to the grief process.

Prayer for Consolation

Bring me your consolation.
Comfort me.
I need the sweet balm of your assurance.

This burden is heavy
And I stagger under the load.
If I fail, all will be lost.
Console me with your strength.

Bring me your consolation.
Comfort me.
I need the soft light of your guidance.

The path ahead is dim
And I'm not sure where to step.
If I lose my way, many will suffer.
Console me with your light.

Oh, bring me, again, your consolation,
Your mighty comfort.
Magnify my strength,
Clarify my vision,
And keep me close by you.

by Gillian Savage, Sydney Australia
www.tirralirra.com

<u>CHAPTER 10</u>

J

JOURNALING

Keeping a journal, a diary, a book, a record, whatever you call it, has enormous benefit after the death of a loved one. First, it's a way to make sense of things. You can revisit the life you lead with your loved one, or attempt to figure some aspects of your life now, even express appreciation, frustration, anger, and confusion. There's something about writing it down that clarifies it.

Secondly, you can get rid of the feelings you don't want to carry by writing them out. There is something about defining your feelings in writing that diffuses them. Feelings of loneliness and feelings of anger alike can be placed securely in a journal. That doesn't mean they won't return, but they will probably lessen when recorded on paper.

Third, you can explore the various facets of your life on paper. The way ahead can be contemplated and examined. There are so many decisions that have to be made. Choices can be investigated all with paper and pen. No one else needs to be part of your writing. It doesn't cost anything and it can help you work your way through the grief process.

Write every day if possible. Start with the thoughts that keep reoccurring—even when you try not to think of them. You will find you can say what you might have been afraid to say aloud. Say it secretly in your journal. You don't have to worry about being strong for anyone. Your journal should be written only for you, so you have complete freedom to be yourself. Make your journal your ever-present friend, one who knows all your thoughts and feelings. Keep it locked in a safe place so that it can be private.

From time to time you can go back and reread what you have written. Amazingly, you will see how you're progressing. There will be setbacks, of course, but the whole journey will be there recorded in a safe place. For many people, writing can be a wonderful therapeutic tool.

A difficult place

I fell into a dark place of difficulty,
Prickles and thorns were uncomfortably everywhere,
and all the glasses were half-empty.
I didn't want what I could have
and I couldn't have what I wanted.

My pencil lay idle in my hand
as I looked blankly at the paper.
I shuffled my feet and looked across the garden.
Pleasant.
The deep chimes rang three soft notes,
leaving me unmoved.
So I stay in glum half-animation,
listening for what needs to be said,
I find no response.
What is this hollowness with no voice
that cries mutely for form?

With my pencil, I wait—it seems
that something needs saying.
Fragments of thoughts trail across the surface
and leave no trace.
This heavy formlessness eludes me.
Neither happy nor unhappy, far from joy or despair,
I am caught in bland, dull unknowing.

A whispered memory-line from the Messiah
leaves an eddy in the current—
'Comfort me', it says. The ripple repeats
and swells to a fragile pattern,
'Comfort me, bring me your consolation.'
My pencil moves tentatively
and I have found what needs to be said.

by Gillian Savage, Sydney Australia
www.tirralirra.com

JOY

Survivors may find themselves feeling guilty when they enjoy something and find themselves laughing. You may have trouble giving yourself permission to be happy, especially in a public place.

But joyful moments don't mean you're being disloyal to your lost loved one nor are you uncaring and insensitive. It simply means you're normal with a range of human emotions. Of course, at this time, overall, you are sad, but all emotional reactions don't have to be confined to sadness. It isn't wrong to find pleasure again, to laugh and return to a full range of emotions. Allowing yourself normal moments of joy is necessary in grief because those moments of joy help you go on with your life.

Don't repress the expression of pleasure and don't be afraid to join in the laughter. Instead, be thankful you can still experience this joy. Your loved one wouldn't want you to remain mired in only the deepest and darkest emotions.

A dear friend of mine who enjoys a wonderful sense of humor lost her husband of 40 years. They were childless and particularly close. He sometimes expressed his concern directly to his wife during his long illness and worried how she might carry on without him. They talked about how difficult it would be for her to take care of their large house and how she might manage her affairs.

When he died, his wife sifted through his papers and found the following poem. Through this poem her loving husband helped her to go on in a positive way. It was his permission to be joyful; it was his final gift to her.

To those I love

If I should ever leave you whom I love
To go along the Silent way, grieve not,
Nor speak of me with tears;
But laugh and talk
Of me as if I were
Beside you there.
(I'd come—I'd come,
could I but find a way!)
But would not tears and grief
Be barriers.
And when you hear a song
Or see a bird
I loved, please do not let
The thought of me
Be sad . . . For I am

Loving you just as
I always have . . .
You were so good to me!
There are so many things
I wanted still
To do—so many things
To say to you . . .
Remember that I
Did not fear . . . It was
Just leaving you
That was so hard to face . . .

We cannot see Beyond . . .
But this I know:
I loved you so—T'was heaven
Here with you!

by Isla Paschal Richardson

CHAPTER 11

KINDNESS

Acts of kindness are both given and received. In the time of grief it's difficult to focus on the positive when things seem so bleak, but it's gratitude that brings us out of grief.

Being thankful means remembering and acknowledging the acts of kindness that have happened to you. Did someone send flowers? A card or note? Did someone call just to see how you are doing? Those are the things to think about now. These are the points of gratitude that will lift you up as the days go on.

Sometimes when we're in a desperate state we forget the kindnesses and concentrate on the omissions of kindness. "Why didn't Sarah call me when Bill died? I expected to hear from her." Perhaps she should have called and you may feel disappointed not to hear from a dear friend, but for now it's better to dwell on the kindness bestowed on you and be grateful. When we don't hear from someone we assume will call, there's usually a reason. Some people have a difficult time with death. They may be dealing with their own grief issues.

To give is to receive! If you can reach out to another survivor you will help yourself. It's as simple as asking someone in your support group how they're doing. By talking to each other you give to each other and receive healing

After the terrorist bombing of the World Trade Twin Towers in New York City on September 11, 2001, thousands of mourners took to the streets in search of their loved ones. For anyone who watched, it seemed obvious that many family members were on a futile search. Their family member might have been on the very floor where the plane struck the building. But for them searching allowed them to *do* something and it allowed them to be with others who faced the same grief.

When I saw the crowds standing in line, talking to one another, gathering together in the stadium, I knew why they were there. Like me, they simply couldn't stay trapped in their agony. Their grieving process had begun not in isolation but by breaking out of it. By "giving solace" the survivors were themselves receiving solace in a situation that seemed beyond anyone's comprehension.

There's a time for isolation and a time when reaching out is your only means of survival! Survivors are bound together and it's in acts of kindness to each other that we survive. Reaching out to another survivor is never inappropriate. It may not be the conventional avenue of contact but it's never wrong when done in good faith.

CHAPTER 12

L

LOSS

When we lose a loved one, we lose more than a single person. We lose the plan of our life and the dream that gives us hope and energy. Without that dream it seems so difficult to move forward. It seems that the loss cancels out all that we cling to, all that sustains us, all that we had hoped for, almost all that made life worthwhile and special.

It takes time to reinvent the life we have in front of us. Slowly we can fill in our lives with things that are good for others and ourselves. Perhaps we can make a difference in the world around us but it will take time. The grief journey starts at a new beginning place. There's a whole new world to come to understand and this knowledge can't be acquired in a day.

Loss can create a crisis in self-esteem. The plan of our life has been rearranged and we may feel a sense of worthlessness without our previous goals and visions. Moving on will require a belief in the power of our own spirit.

A time of loss is a time of transition. Remember the past with confidence knowing you handled your life responsibly before and you will again. You're still the same person and your crisis in self-esteem is only temporary. Read the following affirmations each day:

I am just as capable as I once was.
I am just as appealing and important to those around me.
I must not give up on myself.
I must not think I am unworthy of attention, love or reward.
I am a worthwhile person.
I have a lot to offer this world.

On February 21st, every year, Martie Odell-Ingebretson remembers her daughter, Michelle, with her gift of poetry. Her poems have become beautiful paper memories.

February 21, Every Year

Today you emerged
from hibernation.
I felt you tapping
the shoulder
of my memory.

Look, you said,
I am
swept under the heartbeat
of memory, sleeping,
covered by hours
then by days
finally by years
until my laughter
fades from memory
and the sound of my voice
is lost.

I am only noticed
when February cuts into
your heart
or in my picture
one sided and posed.

You look for me
across the mountain top
as if my ashes are what
seed the ground
and I can feel
the pilgrimage
of your feet
upon my soul.

Your heart beat
is me
and the ache
in womb
the full blue veined
breast of remembering
is where you can find me
and I will always be there
trust your tears.

Paper Memories

How could I not write of her
not write of her in February
when her blushed cheeks glowed
and she wanted to wear
those flannel pajamas with feet
all the time

I have her blue blanket
torn and blistered from her dragging
and did you know that it was mine too
put away in tissue and wrapped with love
like brand new when I gave it to her
she took it with her all around
and now it fades away in the box
with the drawings and hand prints
that I cannot look at most times
for I am not brave enough
to count the tears she shed
learning the alphabet
or laughs that are there
in paper memories

I know I build this month
with layers of years and days
of springs and summers when to capture her
is not what I think of every morning
not a wisp of her all day creeps
past good old time that heals all things
except for mothers
and I'm thankful for the wound

It is like her pointing a finger at me
and saying I am still with you
was a part of you
and always always will be there
to drop tinsel on your February
and dance around in the attic of your mind
making footprints that you can feel
with your living

So forgive me all who read again and again
in February of the time so long ago
when youth was mine
and I thought all things were possible
for I cannot not write of her in February
it is all that I have

LEARNING

In the beginning of the grief process, it's a matter of survival. We don't know or care about the learning that automatically happens through the process. Actually, it's probably the last thing on our mind. But then it happens!

The first thing we learn is that we can survive. We find resources within ourselves that we didn't even know existed. These resources once tapped will now serve us throughout the rest of our lives.

The second thing we learn is the real meaning, depth, and scope of love. We recognize fully the necessity for receiving love in our daily lives. We may have some regrets and wish we had expressed our love more fully; we may even be angry at ourselves. But such anger can only be replaced with forgiveness and the determination to allow love to enter our lives again. Perhaps we have gained a new capacity for commitment to those around us. Love becomes a major factor in reshaping our lives.

The final thing we learn is that we have taken on a wisdom—one that only comes as a result of loss. We recognize this wisdom in other survivors and it's centered around the valuing of the very essence of life and having a clearer understanding of life's purpose.

Widow

I keep pruners by the door
to cut flowers for your grave,
in your car a straw hat, a folding chair.
I find the missing Books on Tape,
a French franc under the driver's seat.

I wear your T-shirts to bed,
your shirts with my jeans.
I avoid the dining room,
eat dinner standing at the sink.

I give away your size 13 ski boots,
your left-handed scissors, cling
to the idea that you believe in me
as I learn to relight the pilot,
drive alone at night.

I'm confused when your presence
seems to leave and return at will,
want to learn to manage grief
as easily as I peel this pear.

LOVE

The love you shared with your loved one is a gift—a gift that calls for gratitude. It's the one gift that says you have lived a meaningful life. Love is our most precious commodity.

As with all precious and worthwhile things, love has its price. Sometimes it hurts to have loved and sometimes it hurts even more to have loved deeply. You might now wonder why you couldn't have loved but still protect yourself from all this pain. That's not possible!

Without love, you could withdraw from life and live in an emotionless state by not feeling the joys of life. Would anyone want that? Would you want to have missed being loved and loving in return?

Even though we may feel especially lost and hurt with our loved one gone, we wouldn't wish to erase the love from our lives. When someone loves us, it affirms our worthiness. We are accepted, cherished, and esteemed. So when we lose that person it may seem as though we are no longer important to anyone.

Whenever we lose someone who loved us we are challenged by a crisis in self-love. Simply, we have lost someone whose approval was important to us. Now it's important to seek the support of others who care about us, even though it will never be the way our loved one cared. It's by giving and receiving love that we gradually fill in the void left by this loss of love.

Wind

Winds blow through the forests of the world
and we smell love.

Ocean tides blanket the earth
and we taste love.

Stars and galaxies swing through the sky
and love is ours.

A small bird lights in your garden and calls.

The quiet voice of love surrounds us all.

Love lifts us, binds us, moves us, teaches us, heals us.

And shakes us . . .

© by Gillian Savage, Sydney Australia
www.tirralirra.com

William Shakespeare's Sonnet #116 defines love and explains the nature of love through its divine permanence. He saw love as an ever-fixed mark that is never shaken, even by death. Shakespeare claimed that love doesn't change in time but goes on forever. Love is truly life's greatest gift.

Sonnet #16------

Let me not to the marriage of true minds
Admit impediments. Love is not love
Which alters when it alteration finds,
Or bends with the remover to remove:
O no! it is an ever-fixed mark
That looks on tempests and is never shaken;
It is the star to every wandering bark,
Whose worth's unknown, although his height be taken.
Love's not Time's fool, though rosy lips and cheeks
Within his bending sickle's compass come:
Love alters not with his brief hours and weeks,
But bears it out even to the edge of doom
If this be error and upon me proved,
I never writ, nor no man ever loved.

by William Shakespeare

CHAPTER 13

MOODS

One of the most disarming problems during a time of grief comes in the form of sudden bursts of sadness. These floods of emotion may come and go very quickly like the ocean tides ebbing and flowing. Just as they push forward into our world, they quickly fall away. These sudden feelings are as normal as the natural flow of the tides.

Usually our grief stays out of our conscious thoughts most of the time, but it remains with us to some degree. These sudden emotions are evidence that external people, places, and things can trigger pain.

There seems to be no rhyme or reason to the placement of the moods; they just develop. A grieving widow will begin to cry at the bank or post office. She remembers stopping by every other day with her husband. A grieving father will cry at a friend's daughter's wedding when he thinks of the wedding his daughter will never have. A daughter will hear a song on the radio. It was the song her father used to whistle. She will cry driving down the highway. There's no preparation for these sudden bursts of sadness. They just happen.

Mood swings are actually beneficial because they allow you to process the grief a little at a time. Can you imagine how terrible it would be to experience the loss all at once?

As time passes the sad moments will occur with less and less frequency. In the midst of these moments remember to let it happen knowing you will gain your composure and become fully engaged a bit later.

You might feel disappointed in yourself because you can't seem to control your emotions. Perhaps it embarrasses you. You might even wonder when all this sadness will go away. You might even wonder if you are just a depressive type, wallowing in the emotion of the moment.

I used to wonder about the sadness I held inside. It wasn't until I realized that it's normal to have a sad place inside that I was able to get over the shame I felt about mood swings. I had to come to understand that it's not because I'm not healed that I go back to sadness. It's because I still and always will have a reserve of devotion for the ones I've loved and lost. This reserve of devotion is the evidence of the love we shared.

By making peace with the sad place inside and welcoming the healthy emotions that come out of that place, I now feel a deeper sense of emotional peace.

MEMORIES

Our memories are so important! They keep us going, give us strength, and can be passed on to others who cared about our loved ones. Memories are important because they can never be taken from us. They are our own private and unique collection that we can return to at will.

Because memories are so precious, we fear that we will lose them. Exacerbating that fear is the fact that memories do dim in time. You might be afraid that you won't be able to recall a certain look, habit, or gesture—something your loved one said or the way they said it. Fearing the loss of a memory can sometimes hasten the dimming of it.

The best way is to keep the memories alive. You can do that by recording on tape, or in a journal. Record the things your loved one said, or the way he/she looked or acted. You can list the special moments, times you most enjoyed together. You can assemble notes, photographs, letters, and clippings in one place. This place can become the memory bank where you can visit anytime. You might ask others to share their tributes as well.

We can't eliminate the difficult memories that seem to surface from time to time. When you feel you're overwhelmed by a bad image or memory, picture yourself opening up another section of your memory bank where all the loving memories are stored. Consciously steer yourself back to the loving ones. Go to your journal, look at a favorite picture and be uplifted by the good. You can't stop unpleasant images, but you don't have to dwell in them.

As a high school teacher, I've experienced the death of many young people. Some from suicide, traffic accidents, and murder. Some I knew very well; some I knew through other young people. One thing I always noticed about teens who grieve is that they record the good memories in some significant way.

Almost immediately students would begin every sentence with "I remember when." Then they would choose a symbolic place to bring their flowers, pictures, poems, and tokens of their memories. It might be a special place in school, or a tree on the side of the road.

I can remember vividly one very cold morning in the December snow of New England going to the side of a country road to write an inscription on a wooden cross. "To the big guy—from Mrs. A." The big guy's girlfriend was with me—she stood back and wept uncontrollably. Other kids from my class gathered to put their last words on Andy's cross. No one arranged this meeting; no one said, "instead of English class let's meet there at this place," or "let's write down our thoughts on this rough cross." We just moved together in memory. Instinctively, young people—grieving people—know what to do.

RAIN

That Spring,
the silence of death came,
in the middle of the night, and
there were dirges sung.

Droning like a brown covered beetle,
whimpering like a wounded sparrow,
as bare trees bore no blossoms, and
and sap bled from the maple branches.

We cried with the rain that spring.

That summer—
The heaviness of life came in the middle
of the day, and there were useless ditties to
be sung, with croaking undisciplined frogs.
Chirping like wrens, as willows drooped
in the sun. Pressing us into frivolity.
Making us cry again!

Like summer flowers, our hearts re-opened
and the rain mingling with our tears,
washed us clean once again.

MEANING

When we lose someone precious, we may feel a sense of hopelessness making things seem meaningless. Death with its finality has a way of conveying that message. You have a choice: "what's the use of living?" or "I wish to live more fully."

Trying to understand why death happens or what life really means can be frustrating. We don't need to have the answers to the big questions in order to continue meaningful lives. All we have to do is look at the balance in the natural world and we can see that change is the only constant in life—and life and death are part of all natural things. Anyone who grows a garden or lives surrounded by nature knows the cycle of life and death.

Sometimes when we grieve we might forget that every small task of everyday life is part of the total harmony of the universe. Sometimes it seems that our existence is totally unimportant. We might think that because we are not making some remarkable contribution our lives are meaningless.

Nothing is further from the truth! The work of grieving is important even if it involves getting through one moment at a time. Whatever you do now, it's important, however insignificant it may seem. For some it may mean just getting up in the morning and getting dressed. It may mean just facing the day as it unfolds. Every small task has its place in the overall order of things. You might argue that you could stop everything you do and no one would notice. How do you know that? Perhaps there is someone who understands your grief and sees you carrying on and that gives them the courage to face the day and carry on too.

You say the world would not come to an end without you, but your contribution, through your actions, is part of the active world. What you do is important because it contributes to the life processes of those around you.

* * *

Her name was Sarah. I met her at the Writer's Conference in Maui, Hawaii. Sarah, a young attractive woman, one of the major editors with a New York publishing house, was interviewing me.

When she saw I had written a book called *Gratitude Therapy* she asked, "How can you be grateful for *everything*?"

"Well, usually some good comes from bad. There's always a reason to be grateful." I countered.

"Like a death?" she continued.

I hesitated wondering where this was going.

"Yes, I believe that's true."

"But how can you find good in let's say the death of a child?" Her face changed and I knew she was talking about her child.

"That's the worst situation imaginable." I said looking away, "but I know some people can come out of it and find new meaning. I had a child that died."

"So did I."

"How old was your child?"

"Four years old—and I don't know what it means."

Images of a small child flooded my mind and I felt the deepest pain. Tears welled up and I couldn't find any more words about gratitude. There was silence! In that quiet moment there was a connection of mother's hearts—both of us had suffered the same loss.

Remembering where she was, Sarah recouped, wrote her name and address on a small white piece of paper and said, "Write a handbook for those who have lost a loved one." The interview was over; she was gone. The idea for this book was born.

Since my brief but poignant meeting with Sarah, I have thought about her and what I wished I could have said. Later, I realized she herself brought meaning to the death of her child. Here she was, a productive, talented woman who helped people like me write books for those who grieve. Her very existence made a statement for life! It was her reason to be grateful!

LIFE IS!

A kaleidoscopic lithograph—
with its ever changing patterns:
Phobic shadows, blending into
effervescent shapes.
Growing moments.

Hexagonal, octagonal, diagonal,
sifting, switching, reversing me!
Into lineal, pinnacle, pirouetted places—
spaces moving.

Turn it upside down, I laugh out loud:
Turn it inside out, I cry.

A kaleidoscopic lithograph—
with its ever-changing colors:
sharp reds, touching mellow blues,
And blacks, blacks, too.
Rhythmic moments!

Turn it toward me, I see birth;
Turn it away, I see death.

Wait!
Now!
Seeing a balance, sensing a rhythm,
I see golden things, butterfly wings.
Soft, mellifluous motions, magic,
reflected illusions of light and dark.

My kaleidoscopic life presents its own
unique perspective,
its own primary colors,
its own special beauty,
It's own meaning!

© by Christine A. Adams

MEMORIALIZATION

When you arrange a memorial service to honor your loved one, you are facilitating the healing process because the service helps you fully recognize the end of your loved one's life on earth. This is a time when you can say goodbye, express your feelings, and review the memories you shared. This service can help you integrate the loss into your present life.

Memorialization of a loved one can be very important to the grievers. Without it, we may feel confused and lost. But what's an appropriate memorial service? There's no set answer to that question. Does it mean a church? Not necessarily. Does it have to be public? Does it have to involve more than one person? Can it take place anytime? These are questions only you can answer.

You may choose not to have a formal memorial service, or your loved one may have specified that they would prefer no memorial service. There are additional ways, beyond a formal service, that may be more appropriate for you. You may conduct a private ceremony that simply happens when it's supposed to happen.

Memorialization can become more than a single event. Sometimes, in an ongoing way we memorialize by letting go of the old roles as we take on new ones. A son may memorialize his father when he takes on his new role as patriarch of the family. A daughter may carry out her mother's dream, a parent may become active in an organization that helps other survivors.

We also memorialize with material objects. A monument at the gravesite is a visible sign of your loved one's earthly existence. A material possession, which may mean nothing to someone else, could become a memorialized treasure to be cherished forever.

Sometimes a memorialized treasure can be passed on to another person. As a teacher, this happened to me. I had a student who was suicidal. Her preoccupation with death was evident in her poetry. As her English teacher, I was able to give her extra credit for writing a book of poetry, take off some of the stress of the regular curriculum, and keep more closely in touch. She confided in me.

That year my mother died. She had been a registered nurse and insisted that she take care of herself in her own home until the last moment of her life. When the pain of the cancer became difficult, her doctor prescribed Demerol. Just as she had done as a nurse, she kept a record of her own meds. When she died we found a small card beside her bed. Written in her hand, was "I took Demerol at 9A.M., at 2 P.M." She was recording so that she didn't overdose. Sometime after 2 P.M. she died of natural causes.

When I saw that card, I knew it represented my mother's incredible fortitude. It also represented her wish *not* to take her own life even in the face of a debilitating cancer. I carried that card with me for strength.

However, when my suicidal student was about to graduate, I knew I needed to help her go on. On her last day, I took out the small card, told her what it meant, and asked her to look at it when she needed strength. She promised she would. Years later, I got a letter from her. In the letter was the small card. She confided that she had always relied on it for strength but that now she was sure she was safe and no longer needed it. I learned later that she became a teacher, too.

Many survivors feel the need to keep certain personal effects—the objects they most related to their loved one. One woman who lost her husband when she was in her sixties still had her husband's beautiful cashmere coat in the closet. She had gone on to live a full life and was now in her eighties. Somehow, even though she felt she should give the coat away, she couldn't part with that coat. She told me she remembered the day he bought it, the look on his face, his delight. Her husband's coat had become a symbolic memorial to him.

Makeshift memorials are just as important as planned ones. A cross can be placed on a tree beside the highway. Pictures of those lost in the Oklahoma bombing were placed on a fence that became a makeshift memorial until a real one could be constructed. The students of Columbine were quick to put up their notes, poems, and favorite pictures of fellow students. The entire British nation became the site of makeshift memorials in the days following Diana's death.

Setting Up a Memorial Tribute Online

Many counselors agree that one of the key tasks for the grieving person is to memorialize his/her loved one so that he/she can move on. There are many ways to memorialize your loved one through the Internet. One idea is to attach a memorial page to an existing site. Some unusual personal sites provide on-line memorials where you light a virtual candle, listen to music, or put in a favorite picture of your loved one. The value of these personal remembrances is that you can return to them anytime you want—day or night.

Many pages are offered free. But be sure you understand the terms of the agreement before setting up the tribute. If you post a tribute, be aware that things can change rapidly on the net and sites can go down without notice.

Making a Special File

One way to guarantee that your tribute will be permanent is to incorporate it into your own Web page. Many Web servers (GTE, Earthlink, or Sprint) offer a free personal site. You might link a dedication page to your own site.

Another possibility is to download special quotes, poems, or articles from various sites into a permanent file. Your file could also contain a journal that you enter as you accept the reality of the death, experience the pain of your grief, and adjust to life without the deceased. However, in no way should the Internet take the place of "one on one" grief counseling, sharing with friends, family, or church members, or other forms of traditional grief processing. The Internet should be a useful supplementary tool.

MYTHS

The Five Common Myths About Grief

Myth #1: Grief and mourning are the same experience.

There is an important distinction between them. We have learned that people move toward healing not just by grieving, but through mourning, the actuality of the grief.

Myth #2: There is predictable and orderly stage-like progression to the experience of mourning.

That stage-like thinking about both dying and mourning has been appealing to many people. We understand that different people die in different ways, and likewise, each person mourns in his or her own way, too.

Myth #3: It is best to move away from grief instead of toward it.

Many grievers, unfortunately, do not give themselves permission or receive permission from others to mourn, to express their feelings. We continue to live in a society that often encourages people to prematurely move away from their grief instead of toward it. The result is that many people either grieve in isolation or attempt to run away from their grief.

Myth #4: Following the death of a loved one, the goal is to "get over" your grief.

We've all heard it, "Have you gotten over it yet?" Or the even cruder comment, "Well now, shouldn't he be over it by now?" To think we "get over" our grief is presumptuous. For the mourner to assume that life will be exactly as it was prior to the death is unrealistic and potentially damaging.

Myth #5: Tears expressing grief are only a sign of weakness.

Unfortunately, many people associate tears of grief with personal inadequacy and weakness. Yet crying is nature's way of releasing internal tension in the body and allows the mourner to communicate a need to be comforted.

Only when we as a society are able to dispel these myths of grief will grieving people experience the healing they deserve!

by Alan D. Wolfelt, Ph.D.
Director of the Center for Loss and Life Transition
Thanatos, Fall 1989, pp. 25-27

CHAPTER 14

NIGHTS

The nighttime seems to be particularly difficult for most survivors. It can produce dreams, nightmares, and sometimes visions. Dreams might seem pleasant when you imagine your loved one alive and well, participating in some enjoyable activity. Yet, dreams can become nightmares when you replay some difficult scene as you might after a tragic accident or protracted sickness. Sometimes survivors believe their loved ones have returned in dreams to let them know that they are all right.

Dreaming about your loved one is normal but disconcerting. Just as you are beginning to realize that the loss has occurred, your dreams present them as an alive and well person. Just as you feel yourself healing from the trauma of tragedy or sickness, the feelings return.

Although dreaming is normal, it's not abnormal if you don' t have these dreams. We all process our grief in different ways. Some people need to filter their grief through the subconscious and they do so in their sleep.

In addition to dreams and nightmares, it's not uncommon for survivors to have visions, imagining they are in the presence of their loved one. These experiences are not fully explained but could be the product of our subconscious minds, making what we so fervently wish for seem to be happening. There are no scientific reasons for paranormal experience. They just seem to happen.

If, during an intense period of grief, you imagine you have had a visit from the spirit of your loved one, even hearing his/her voice, don't be alarmed. You're not losing your mind. Many other survivors have experienced the same visions. However, if these visions persist, it's time to get help.

Even if you never dream, have nightmares, or have visions, the nights can be particularly difficult for you. It's the time when you come face to face with your grief. During the day there may be distractions, but at night the reality of the death seems ever present. It will take time to adjust to nighttime!

Some people just can't seem to shut off their minds and drift off to sleep. Many people take some medication to sleep in the early days. A bit of prudence is advised here because eventually you will have to face your grief in the quiet of your bedroom. To delay this reality with heavy medication is only putting off the inevitable and perhaps causing a situation that could be addictive. Whenever we use a chemical substance to avoid our pain, we may be on dangerous ground.

Alcohol can be used to deaden the feelings of grief much in the same way. Many widowers who became alcohol dependant after the loss of a spouse admit they used alcohol to dull the pain and put them to sleep at night. Again, alcohol is a depressant and a mind-altering drug, so when taken in heavy doses it will slow down bodily systems and cause a heavy sleep. Prolonged reliance on alcohol is dangerous and will cause serious problems.

Then, how can you cope with the nights? First, be prepared by recognizing that the nighttime is usually the most difficult time. Be prepared for some very difficult times at first. Next, slow down your schedule so that you can catch up on your sleep if you need to. Try sleeping in a different location. In time, the nights will become more bearable. Finally, have faith in yourself and be patient. One night you will fall off to sleep just like you used to before this loss.

Hollow

A tactile basin sunken deep
beneath the mountain's ridge caress
left space like naked wilderness;
a place for memories to keep.

~ ~ ~

Though the brilliant sunlight beamed,
no splendid greening grass would grow.
No crocus swelled beneath the snow,
although the moonlight's sheen yet gleamed.

~ ~ ~

And sorrow's grey lies down to weep,
for night has crawled across the field.
No comfort will this evening yield,
no gentleness to help me sleep.

NUMBNESS

Sometimes everything feels unreal. It seems as if we're floating through the day, going from one necessary task to another, seeing a person here and there—sometimes with no recall of what has happened.

The feeling of being adrift, of being cut loose, set apart from our normal experiences persists. The demands of our life seem more than we can bear at this time. But our resilience is strong and we survive in our numbness.

The sense of unreality, of being disconnected from the world, is to be expected. It shouldn't last long. Gradually you will feel more connectedness, more stability. The numbness and the floating feeling will dissipate and a whole range of feelings will take their place. The mind and body are taking care of themselves in their own way. A sense of disconnectness protects the mind from the full blow of your loss. All you need to do is accept the numb feelings as normal and wait for them to gradually subside.

The Dance of Grief

Take three steps forward and 2 steps back,
Spin round in a circle 'till you forget where you're at.
Fall down in a heap and get up again,
Get your bearings straight, then start again.

This is the dance, the dance of grief,
Prepare yourself, 'cause it won't be brief.
Each time you think you're nearing the end,
Something happens and you have to begin again.

But one day, the time will arrive,
When only your memory dances, and you have survived.
Your body moves on with the life it must live,
But your memory never forgets, the dance that you did.

CHAPTER 15

OBSESSIVE THOUGHTS

Sometimes when we're alone, we keep reviewing the same things over and over again. These obsessive thoughts might be images that flashback, conversations we keep rehearsing, or other painful thoughts and feelings that seem to stay with us no matter how hard we try to rid our minds and hearts of them.

We might question the loss of our loved one. Condemn ourselves in anger or condemn others. Sometimes we think there's some particular information that we desperately need to talk over with our loved one. Sometimes there's a recurring dream with the same haunting theme. Tormenting, obsessive thoughts!

Here are some ways to handle obsessive thoughts:

1. Acknowledge the thought by expressing it to someone you trust or to a professional. Somehow talking about the obsession weakens it.
2. If you can't talk about it, write it down. Write out each detail describing the hurt, guilt, confusion, or outrage. The more detailed the description, the more power you give it on paper and the less power it has over you!
3. Examine your writing and you may find that your thoughts have taken a new turn. Now you can add to it, take it apart, and understand it. Finally, you will feel as if you are getting some control over it.
4. Use positive self-talk to ward off negative self-talk. Counter the negative with the positive by saying to yourself, "I am a child of God and I doing the best I can this day."

5. If you are plagued by a recurring guilt, anger, or confusion—one that is holding you back—give that feeling to God. Visualize these sources of pain and anguish being taken up to God. Visualize yourself handing that anger or guilt over to someone who can handle it better than you can. Let it go! Just for now! Just for this moment! Then, let the peace of God settle over you for a moment. You may not be able to give up your anger or guilt permanently, but you can take a rest from it for awhile.

CHAPTER 16

PROCRASTINATION

It's natural to procrastinate when you're grieving. The energy is simply not there. You might be preoccupied with your own thoughts and less able to concentrate. Phone calls, errands, shopping, correspondences, chores, and work-related tasks can pile up. When we think of all we have to do, it seems insurmountable so we procrastinate because we don't know where to start.

Whenever I am dealing with grief or some other crisis in my life, I give myself permission to live in "survival mode." I ask, " What do I need to do today to survive?" By putting the emphasis on the basics—just the *most* important things—I am able to reduce that insurmountable pile of "things to be done" and just do what is necessary.

Some survival days may be extremely simple—get up, take a shower, get dressed, go to work, come home, sit quietly and think, read or write, eat, and then go back to bed. However, if survival means I need to pay the rent or phone bill, I will probably have to do that paperwork so I can survive the next day. But, everything that can be delayed will be.

Sometimes it helps to make a list of things we need to do, just the things that are necessary right now. Aside from what's required to earn a living and keep us going financially, there's usually a lot of room for procrastination. This is the time to go easy on you, to give yourself permission just to survive.

Expecting yourself to be as efficient as you were before the death is unrealistic and frustrating. This is the time to ask for help from friends and family as you need it. There are some things that will seem too hard to do because they bring back memories that are painful. Turn to a friend or relative and become willing to accept their help. Do only what you need to do to survive in the early days; and your strength will return more quickly.

Looking

I feel like there is something I should do,
But I can't remember what.
I walk around aimlessly looking for it,
But whatever it was, I guess I forgot.
There's heaps of things that I could do,
But I don't want to do them.
I walk around and I sit down,
Then I stand and walk again.
Something I read the other day said,
That I'm subconsciously looking for my baby.
I was glad when I read that,
'Cause I thought I was going crazy.

© by Sharon Swinney, Gleneagle, Australia

PERSEVERANCE

This time of grief may be the most challenging time of your life, but you can persevere. Think of other challenging times in your life. Where did you find the strength to persevere then? What personal resources did you turn to then? If you had the resources then, it's likely you still have the strength to persevere.

Even though we're not called upon to endure great difficulties each day, we all possess within us strong, raw, resilient material to survive. Perhaps this is your most challenging test—a test that will demand strength untapped before.

A survivor needs to know everyday that they can draw from the sources inside themselves, and that these resources won't run out. They need to believe that they can make it through and survive this loss. Look at your past challenges and let that inspire you, or take inspiration from others who have endured great loss.

> Human misery must somehow have a stop. There is no wind that always blows a storm.
>
> *Euripides* (422 B.C.)

During this time it's normal to think there's no end to the pain. It's almost impossible to imagine the situation can change. But it always does! Finally! All things change in time.

When you think you can't stand the pain any longer, sit quietly and comfortably by yourself. Close your eyes and relax your body. Remind yourself that times of relief always follow times of despair. Remember that every day spent in emotional pain will likely be followed by a day of solace. It was like this in the past and will be like this now.

Usually after a storm comes a period of calm. There seems to be a reprieve that leads to sunny days. Yet somehow, when we are in the midst of that storm, we can't think of those sunny days. When we are so sad, we can't think of being happy again. But happiness is not something we can just will into existence.

> Sorrow makes a man think of God.
>
> *Paul Brunton* (1994, p. 201)

Some people find that a faith in the strength of God supplements their own strength and when human doubts and fears enter in, they turn in prayer asking for help from a higher spiritual source. Wherever you need to go to find your strength, go there at this time. Many have found solace in this well-known prayer for guidance.

Prayer of St. Francis of Assisi

Lord, make me an instrument of your peace.
Where there is hatred, let me sow love;
Where there is injury, pardon;
Where there is doubt, faith;
Where there is despair, hope;
Where there is darkness, light
And where there is sadness, joy.

O Divine Master,
grant that I may not so much seek to be consoled
as to console;
to be understood as to understand;
to be loved as to love.
For it is in giving that we receive;
It is in pardoning that we are pardoned,
and it is in dying that we are born to eternal life.

PATIENCE

It's difficult to think of patience as an action because it seems so passive to just wait. But by forcing ourselves to wait we are doing something. We are getting through challenging times in our life.

The kind of strength needed in this period of grief is not the kind that says "I'll smile and keep going." Rather, it's the tenacity that says "I'll wait this out. I'll be patient."

No matter how many times you may have to relive the same emotions or become plagued by feelings of devastation and fear, your patience can carry you through. Your patience can remind you that this moment is only a part of the process of grief and there is an end to the process if you can be patient. By remaining patient, you maintain your power over the process.

Sometimes you might feel impatient and wonder if things shouldn't be changing faster. If you give into this feeling of impatience, becoming angry and demanding change, you will only delay the process.

The progression in your grief process is so individual that it can't be prescribed. There is no formula, no way to say "I should be over this by now!" It's a matter of surviving each day, allowing our responses to our loss to come as they may. We need to patiently trust that if we experience our feelings as they come and let them happen, we will eventually pass through the roughest time.

People will tell you to take one day at a time, one step at a time. Just concentrate on the next right thing. That's good advice because it asks us to concentrate on the present and not look back at the past or too far ahead in the future.

Taking an emotional inventory every day is counter productive because we might improve one day and slip back the next. If we assess ourselves too frequently, we may feel we are not making any headway at all and feel desperate.

PROGRESS

Sometimes in the early days of grieving, we need to keep in motion. We might throw ourselves into our work. By just going from one thing to another and not really accomplishing very much, our job can become a retreat from our feelings. We may tackle work-related problems rather than experience grief-related problems.

There's nothing harmful about this approach if it's temporary. Actually, some survivors may be saving themselves from emotional pain that's too difficult to bear. But no one can escape forever.

Until grief is faced, expressed, and fully experienced, little progress will be made.

After a period of frenzied activity, there needs to be a time when you can take time to look at where you really are. A time to take an emotional inventory. In this inventory, you might consider how you really feel, what you need, and what things you might have been neglecting. The little details of life can distract you for awhile but ultimately these details also keep you away from the care of your spirit and that's where your grief will be ultimately solved.

One of the things most of us who grieve think about is how short life is. Our own mortality has been made more evident by the death of a loved one. Now all lives seem less permanent, including our own.

We may stand back and look at the generations that will follow us. Life will take on a new perspective. So now it's time to think about how you will use your time to enhance the quality of your life and think about the effect you might have on the next generation.

Death brings life into focus and allows us to identify our most valuable assets—the non-material assets. We might make important decisions about our future lives. We might make a decision to turn away from the material world to a more compassionate existence. We might decide to dedicate ourselves to service of others by becoming one who gives more, supports more, and nurtures more. Reflection may bring new resolve and a clearer vision to your life.

But how do you know you are healed? It doesn't happen all at once. In fact, it happens so slowly at first that you may not see any visible signs of healing. But even though you think you're not progressing, you are! Your healing is invisible as your mind and heart slowly become accustomed to your loss, as you continue to reflect, make changes, and continue to live in a changed way.

A Better Place

Cry for me no more
 the many tears of sadness
My time in this world was over
 and it came for me to pass.

Bring the photos of old time
 and see them not with tear-filled
 eyes.

But with eyes of joy and laughter
 and smile once more with me.

Know that I am in a better place
one without disease
without hatred and without death
This kingdom I now call home

I wait here for you
When your time comes to pass
to ease the transition
from the old to the new.

Cry for me no more.
Remember only the laughter.
For I am in another realm
And I wait to see you again.

Happiness comes through the process. It comes through our way of being, our dedication to ourselves and our recovery, and our ultimate acceptance of life as it is with its pain and sorrow. As we go through each day, we need not try to reach happiness as a destination but rather live life as a journey, accepting what comes each day. When we are able to let some sunshine in, our pain will lessen. When we are able to find some meaning in the death, we will feel the pain lesson. Sometimes it helps to simply accept that there might be a higher plan—one that we don't understand.

Remember, Sarah?

Remember, Sarah, when we
held hands tight at the ocean-side
as I tried to explain why your dainty little feet
were being pulled out to sea with sucking sand,
at the same time as water was rushing

us in toward the shore?
Remember your
wonder?

And Sarah, remember
when we talked in the night in
our sleeping bags about the night, stars
and moon, and where had the sun gone, and how
could the world be that huge, and God's
power and love for us so great!
Remember your
fascination?

Oh, Sarah Joy, remember
your saving of shells and seaweed,
kelp, rocks and grasses; everything
was so beautiful to you! Oh,
mommy, keep this for me
until we get home! The

dash was always
stuffed with
piquantly
scented
treasures
* * *
We
were blessed
with six priceless
years
* * *
Remember
how you told me you
wished we had time to live time
over again, so we could have
all our fun again here?

Ah, sweetheart, I too
could have had
no greater
wish.
* * *
Now,
my precious
daughter, it seems to me a
very long time until Heaven. But we'll
be there together. We'll sit at the feet of Jesus,
and He'll tell us all about everything. It will be all perfect joy;
better than any Thanksgiving or Christmas here. And
your sweetness, earnestness, your giggles
and kisses, and our love for each
other will be there for us
to keep

forever.

CHAPTER 17

QUESTIONING

Any time of transition is a time of questioning. Grief is a time of transition, bringing a flood of questions. Like the mother who questions the meaning of life when she loses a sixteen year old in a tragic accident; like the widow who questions why her husband had to leave her just a month after he retired; like the fourteen year old who questions the loss of her father while she still has a lifetime to share with him. There are always questions.

However, no matter how intently we search for answers to these questions they are not to be found outside of us. The answer usually comes from a source deep within ourselves. Often, we ask the questions but instinctively know the answer.

For example, a mother who has lost her teen in a terrible accident will question the meaning of life when she thinks of such a brief life—ended before it really starts. But the answer usually comes when she realizes how meaningful that short life was to her and others. It was so precious and no matter how great her grief, she is grateful for the years she had.

In a time of grief everything is unstable. We question our very thoughts and actions. Should I leave her room the way it was? Should I have done more? Is it right to feel this way? Should I go to the cemetery so much? Should I do more to memorialize my loved one?

Don't be impatient with your questioning. It's a natural part of your grief process. You have a right to grieve in your own way and a right to question. Find a good friend who will be patient with you and who understands that in time you will find your own answers.

Why Is It?

Why is it that when pine trees bleed
their fragrant scent and pine cone seed
in showers round me in the fall
I miss you most of all?

Perhaps because the summer's gone,
and slowly winter's coming on.
Its lowering gloom appears to feed
my ever piercing need.

While waving arms of needles fly
against the paling autumn sky,
your arms my heart keeps longing for
and won't know ever more.

www.crossingrivers.com

CHAPTER 18

REALITY

One of the major tasks for anyone who has lost a loved one is finding their way back to reality. Nothing seems real for such a long time that it's difficult to imagine a world of reality. The most unreal thing in grief is always the actual loss of your loved one. There may be times when you convince yourself that your loved one will walk in the door any second.

The reality of the loss can be with you one moment and gone the next. It's only when we distance ourselves from the daily rituals that we shared and detach from the expectations we once had that the loss seems real.

Saying good-bye, over and over again, in so many ways helps to verify the reality of our loss. You might say goodbye to your loved one's picture, you can say goodbye by writing a letter, or you can talk to your support group about the difficulty you are having believing this loss has happened.

There will be many good-byes in the first year and each one is necessary. It takes time to accept as reality that which we so desperately don't want to believe.

In the early days of grief, we may remember our loved one and recall times we had together. If we have a tendency to mythologize our loved one, it doesn't matter. Whether we obscure an actual event, or fabricate a facet of our relationship, it doesn't matter. What we remember becomes a new reality consisting of the selective memories we wish to keep as we survive this loss. It's all a part of survival.

No one can tell you what memories to keep. Others may try to correct you at times. Let them keep their own set of memories. You don't need to worry about remembering things accurately or looking at the whole picture when you are recollecting precious moments—there is a new reality now.

Winter in Gray

I am winter
Gray and warped is my weathered spirit
Like old boards lying in the rain,
By too many cold seasons in the flat wet countryside.
My hopes echo in a secret lonely cavern, camouflaged
By public smiles of shimmeringly hopeful mirage.

~ ~ ~

I find myself in a hollowed land scooped deep
Into the dark earth like a moldy damp root cellar
In Northern British Columbia.
Haunted by decades of memories—
Leaning tender yearnings, bending like old, cold
Willow branches to the ground, shrouded with emptiness.

~ ~ ~

Painting bright laughter, painstakingly
Disguising wet lids with curving lips;
Masquerading over oils of sorrow on the canvas of life.
I'm lost in my own wilderness.
Imprisoned in the penitentiary of the lifetimes of our past.

© by Rosemary J. Gwaltney
www.crossingrivers.com

RELIGION

Religion is a word that means many things to many people. It can embody meaningful rituals that are performed in community, or alone; it can embody the tenets that guide you in your life and provide the foundation of your faith. For some, the word "religion" has a negative connotation—a series of meaningless rituals that do not embody basic beliefs and have nothing to do with faith or spirituality. Therefore, when someone dies, religion may or may not be a consideration.

Historically, religion has played a decided part in the funeral process. A thousand years before Christ, the ancient Egyptians collected and stored every imaginable personal item—household goods, jewelry, furniture and weapons—so that the deceased might have these things in the afterlife. On the walls of the crypts were sketched glorious pictures of a happy life in the afterlife. Their religious beliefs about death seemed to dominate their life here on earth.

It is believed that Christ rose from the dead and reappeared in human form; thus, he confirmed man's immortality forever and became the savior of many believers. Christians believe they will be reunited with Christ, their savior, in heaven.

About six hundred years after Christ, with the birth of the prophet Mohammed in 570 A.D., the Moslem religion grew in strength through the rise to power of the Islamic nation. The core of their belief centers around one God. "There is no God but one God" is the prayer first spoken by Mohammed and often recited by the Moslems. One fourth of the world's population is divided into two major Moslem sects.

Christianity has split into many sects over the years. The Church of Rome is not the same as the Byzantine Orthodox Church. In the1600s, King Henry VIII of England broke with the Catholic Church of Rome and created the Anglican Church of England, known today in America as the Episcopal Church. Generally, this Protestant Revolution took place during this Renaissance Period and many new religious were formed—Presbyterian, Lutheran, Calvinist, etc. Although these religious groups have different names and sometimes a different body of faith, they all express belief in the existence of God and the afterlife.

So from the ancient times, religious beliefs have dominated our culture and changed our view of death by projecting the possibility of a life after death. In that sense, religion does affect the way we grieve.

A memorial service, which commemorates and finalizes the death and reminds survivors of religious beliefs, can be comforting to those who grieve. The beliefs that one ordinarily attaches to religion like a belief in God and life after death can bring solace to a survivor at this difficult time. However, at this delicate time, you can't force upon the survivor a strong belief in God or an afterlife. Those beliefs are usually established long before the loss occurs. A strong religious background can be helpful during this time of loss but in no way can it be prescribed for those who grieve.

REGRETS

Regrets are normal for anyone who grieves. There are always things we didn't have a chance to do. You might wish you had made a move to another place, taken an earlier retirement, taken more family vacations, had a child sooner, attended more important events in the life of your loved one, or taken a more active part in the life of your brother or sister. Regrets. How do we deal with them?

Remember there was a reason why you didn't make that move, retire earlier, take more vacations, or have a child sooner. They were good reasons at the time. Perhaps you could have been move active in someone's life but most of us do the best we can with what we have to deal with at any given time. You did the best you could at that time.

Regrets can consume you if you don't make a decision to also consider the good choices you made, and the pleasurable moments you shared. There must be a conscious decision to balance your regrets with a consideration of your accomplishments and pleasures.

Life can never be all one way or the other. So, try not to second guess yourself. You can protect yourself from being overwhelmed with regrets when you counterbalance these feelings of remorse with worthwhile recollections.

If you really feel that you must change a pattern of your life, then let this loss be the catalyst for change. Spend more time with those you love, be more daring in your decisions, think ahead and plan your life with an eye for the future. Regrets that just linger and haunt us are different from regrets that prompt us to act in a different way in the future. Make any regrets you might have work for you rather than defeat you.

Scattered Echoes

Flowers for a grave,
Both dainty and distressing,
As tears escape twin rivers of the soul.
Convenient time I gave,
Infrequently expressing,
The sentiment between routine and role.
Words left unspoken,
Considered unnecessary,
Sunshine and shadows, petals and tears.
Now the bridge is broken,
The chance was temporary,
To cross back and stroll through tender years.
Eulogies and regret,
As mysterious as Jade,
I failed to say just what I really meant.
A cemetery debt,
For love that went unpaid,
And greeting cards I never even sent.

© by Todd-Michael St. Pierre

RISK

There are three stages of growth that surround any major loss in life. First, we retract as if to protect ourselves. It's natural to not want to feel any more vulnerable than we already are so we withdraw from life. In the first stage of retraction, there is safety in inertia, indifference, and even denial.

Secondly, there is a stage of hesitation where we are reluctant to commit ourselves to doing anything that might require too much strength, endurance, or time. Our hesitation is normal. Our self-protection at this time serves an important purpose by allowing us time to gather enough strength to stand on our feet again.

The third and final stage comes when we become willing to venture out again and rejoin the world. We return to work, reenter our circle of friends and neighbors, and get back into life. It's at this time that we are most conscious of risk-taking—everything seems risky. New activities, new relationships, new commitments. All very frightening, like anything new and different!

So why do we need to push ourselves to risk? Simply because risk is an inherent part of life. If we're going to live again we must risk—to engage, to connect, to be part of the world again. Not doing so means we take the chance that our lives will be limited, and less meaningful. The wholeness of life itself is at stake in our ability to risk.

Stephanie Mendel describes attending a movie by herself for the first time after the loss of her husband.

Before And After

It was so simple.
You'd come down the aisle
With a tub of popcorn and a Pepsi.
I'd reach for them so that you could find space
for your long legs, take off your jacket.
You'd hold the popcorn between your knees,
your hand would reach for mine.
It was time to make plans:
The farmer's market—who'd wait
in line for coffee, who for bread?
Should we pick up ribs on the way home?
The lights would go out
And your arm would be around me.

Now I pick a seat toward the back
Between two empty ones,
not close to the front where we used to sit.

The theatre is full. A man sits down
next to me. I divide my attention
Between the movie and leaning away from him.
On screen Jim Lovell makes his way home
from an ill-fated mission to the moon.
His wife waits for him.
I take Kleenex from my pocket, careful
Not to brush against the man next to me.
That's when I almost walk out,
but I want to pass this test.

© by Stephanie Mendel

RESOLUTION

There is no direct path through the emotions that make up your loss to this magic place of resolution. Since the grief journey has no clear signs, we long for some kind of road map to guide us through. Resolution comes from the willingness to live the loss, to make the grief journey—one day at a time. Sometimes one moment at a time!

Each day that we grieve, that we deal with the painful feelings is another day added to the passage of our grief. There are no clear road signs because everyone travels a different road—their own road.

Grief work takes time. Don't torture yourself by constantly questioning when it will end. Just add one more day to your "Past grief." Concentrate on this day. It's all you have. Don't ignore or minimize the feelings. Relive conversations or events in your mind if you have to. Express regrets and yearnings. If you need to, seek support of others. When grief loses its power over you, it will happen so gradually that you may not recognize it has slipped away.

After my first husband died, I remarried. At that time my new husband and I moved to Central California for a couple of years, so that we could enjoy the climate and live near the ocean. Some days we would walk for miles on the isolated coastline. At first we would bound down the hill leading to the beach, anticipating the solace of the ocean. We would walk to a special place some four or five miles down the beach. The morning sun would cheer us and we would bring a lunch and stay on into the afternoon. Sometimes, on our return trip, a chilly wind would take over, blowing up the sand and pushing us back as we walked. Then, at the end of our trek when we were tired and spent, that formidable hill would be waiting for us.

I learned a trick that I used to get me up that hill when my body was resisting and my mind was saying, "I can't take another step."

I learned to "look down at my feet and never look at the top of the hill." On each labored step, I concentrated on the ground under my feet—soft grey sand, coarse darker grey sand, some black pebbles, more coarse dark grey sand with chunks of tar-like stones.

Then surprisingly I saw the black top of the road and knew I had made it to the top. By checking my progress by the kind of sand beneath my feet, I never had to think about the top of the hill. Somehow I always got there with much less effort than if I kept checking the top of the hill. It just happened!

So, don't ask when will this end. Just concentrate on the matter at hand—the texture of the ground beneath your feet. Somehow, miraculously, if you keep going you will reach the top of the hill. Your grief journey will resolve itself.

Acceptance

At the cliff edge,
each swirling wave
accommodates itself
to the unchanging contours
of impenetrable rock.
In repeat and sighing retreat,
foaming fingers
play their endless symphony
— tender acceptance
of rocky resistance.

The massive lump of shale
endures these attentions
with hunkering fortitude,
immobile
in adamantine acceptance
of this persuasive persistence.

CHAPTER 19

SHOCK

The first wave of shock occurs the moment you discover that your loved one is dead, or going to die. A feeling of numbness sets in and you might feel like you're in a dream. Some people keep thinking they will soon wake up. Some people faint or feel dizzy or nauseated. Anything is possible in this stage, from hysterical tears to being unable to shed a tear. Disbelief is common since the mind simply can't absorb such overwhelming news.

Shock is a protective mechanism, an emotional anesthesia that eases the pain. Your mind can only absorb so much trauma at one time so it goes into this state of numbness and denial to allow the reality of the loss to sink in slowly. The shock response usually lasts from a few hours to a few weeks.

With a prolonged illness, there is a dissipated impact because the shock has been experienced over time. However, no one is ever fully prepared for death. There's no way to avoid the shock, whether it comes all at once or in smaller waves. Loss always produces shock.

After the initial, brutal impact, shock continues with a wave of aftershocks. These aftershocks can leave you in a daze for weeks or months. In this fog, you know on one level that your loved one has died. But on another level you cannot grasp all the ramifications of the loss. Life may seem surreal.

During these aftershocks it's not uncommon to "forget" that your loved one is gone. You might set another place at dinner, you might reach for the phone and dial a number where no one can be reached.

Over and over again you'll come up with the cold reality that your loved one is truly gone.

ALONE IN THE KITCHEN

A solitude that is made of oatmeal
and raisins, and yeast—like yearnings;
settled over my kitchen that morning.

It was in my heart, in my apron pocket,
and in the big wooden spoon that stirred
in the pot.

Like a small yellow daisy
that shared a vase with itself.
I, all alone, set a solitary place
at our table—
realizing for the first time
that you were gone.

© by Christine A. Adams

SADNESS

Crying is nature's way of releasing the stress and helping you heal. Some believe that the tears shed actually help get rid of debilitating toxins in the body. For sure, no one is ever harmed by crying, but stifling their tears has harmed some. So when you have the impulse to express your sadness through tears, don't fight it—just let it happen.

Some people believe that expressions of sadness, or bouts of crying, are signs of weakness. It's true that certain nervous mental states are characterized by incessant bouts of crying. Perhaps we get the notion of weakness from this fact, but the truth is that the expression of sadness is as ordinary as the expression of joy.

Many times our attitude toward tears depends on our culture or childhood experiences. In some cultures crying is seen as a sign of strength of character.

I am a person who is easily moved to tears. A sad movie or a poignant story make me cry. Sometimes I find myself becoming embarrassed when I'm in a public place. I used to be so confused about my ability to be moved to tears that I denied my sad place inside. It had always been my fear that people might see me as overly sad, melancholy perhaps. So I hid the tears.

Then, there came a point of change in my life when I realized that there had been great sorrow in the living of my life and that sorrow made me who I am. Then, I gave myself permission to carry a sad place inside. It wasn't my whole being, it was just a place inside. When I recognized and honored the sad place inside I came to peace with my own uncried tears.

Tears In Rain

What is it about tears
In rain
Those gray shadows casting
Dampened spirits
Across a lamplit street
Forging fingerprints
On oil-slick puddles

What is it about rain
In tears
Stretching ghostly hands
Through a city park
From skeleton trees
Your voice echoing
In the wind

by Rosemary J. Gwaltney
www.crossingrivers.com

SELF-BLAME

Self-blame holds you back from reaching your maximum potential today. It serves no useful purpose to wish you could have been a better daughter, son, mother or father. The time of grief is no time for radical makeovers. However, losing a loved one can be a vehicle of valuable personal insights—ones that will certainly lead to change in time. As your life evolves and your grief diminishes, you can apply what you have learned to your life.

If you do have genuine regrets, remember those regrets can be positive in that they will teach you how to change your life. Prolonged guilt, in and of itself, has no value, except to erode the spirit of the person who carries it. Prolonged guilt can become a comfortable place for some people. We tend to beat ourselves up with a litany of "if onlys." If only I wasn't so irritable when he got sick, if only I knew how much I would miss him, if only I had said "I love you" more often.

None of us can live a perfect life or have a perfect relationship. We are human and have human frailties. When the "if onlys" come to mind, remember you did the best you could with what you were dealing with at that time.

Guilt that prompts us to change might be considered "good guilt." We realize our shortcomings and make a decision to change. We ask God to help remove those shortcomings and move forward. Does that mean perfection at last? Not likely! But it's a positive use of self-blame.

Humility and honesty are the first steps toward spirituality. When we come before a higher power and say, "I made a mistake. Please help me," we are on the path to a new spiritual awareness. Alcoholics Anonymous is a group that uses these principles very effectively. It's only when an alcoholic admits their problem that they are on the way to solving it. Members of that organization have become painfully aware of their humanness through their addiction and reach out to a higher power to help them and guide them. They have decided not to let self-blame destroy them but to transform them.

The serenity prayer is often recited at group meetings but it's helpful to anyone who seeks peace:

> God, Grant me the *serenity*
> To accept the things I cannot change
> The *courage* to change the things I can,
> And the *wisdom* to know the difference.

STRESS

Is stress a part of grief? You can count on that. In order to get back into life, you will have to put up a front and perhaps say you're OK when you're not. Not everyone will know and understand your grief, so you'll have to pick and choose those whom you share with. That's stressful.

You'll have to make important decisions when you are least capable of making them—like where to live, how to pay the bills, how to settle all legal and financial details after the death. These decisions will wear you down because you're both vulnerable and emotionally stressed. That doubles the stress load.

One way to survive the stress load is to find your way to a place of comfort and peace. Some can find peace by prayer and meditation, or taking walks, or being alone in a natural setting. At this stressful time you will probably need a place to "escape to."

One young woman who had just lost her Dad found it difficult to concentrate on her work and respond to the usual office chatter. She decided to skip lunch with the girls for awhile and walk in the park near her work. Here she sat on a bench and ate her lunch alone. This time became precious time for centering her thoughts and relieving the stress of the day. It made it possible for her to get through the afternoon. When she felt better, she rejoined her colleagues, one lunch at a time, until she could join in completely.

You might wonder how often you should take a break from your routine. As often as you need to. Consider these breaks like a release valve that is needed for the inevitable pressure that is building up inside of you. Some days you will need to release more pressure.

Locate your special places, your special times to escape, your release time. Have a plan. Don't wait until the pressure builds and you can't stand it anymore. Take care of yourself in measured, careful steps and soon you'll be able to cope as you did before. If you expect stress during this time and prepare for it, you can reduce it and make life a little more bearable.

Conflict

My heart won't feel the way my head tells it,
    My head says, "Accept it," but my heart won't believe it.
My head says, "You're dying, we have to let you go."
    My heart says, "I still have hope, there could be a miracle you know."
My head says, "You're gone," and I know it is true.
    But my heart still hurts and yearns for you.
My head says, "Come on, pull yourself together."
    My heart says, "I can't, I have too many pieces to gather."
My head says, "Don't cry, keep your tears out of sight."
    My heart says, "I'll try," but then my throat gets tight.
My head says, "You must be strong, You don't want people to see."
    My heart says, "Nick off, I just want to be me."
This is so confusing, which way do I turn?
    I don't know, but this I did learn,
That my head lives on facts and the way it must be.
    But my heart lives on emotions and the way it should be.
You need both to survive in this life.
    But if they could work together, that would be nice.

© by Sharon Swinney, Gleneagle, Australia

SOLITUDE

It's natural to seek solitude when grieving. Times alone are times when we can mull over our innermost thoughts and avoid what may seem like superficial conversations.

Silence serves a valuable purpose now. First, we need to explore what we think and feel about the loss; secondly, we need to think about what we need and hope for. Only in silence can we find these answers.

Many people seek silence in nature, sitting alone by the ocean, hiking in the woods, climbing mountains, or simply listening to the birds sing as you lie on the hammock in the backyard. Finding space to heal, to think, to grow is what quiet times can give you. Kirsti A. Dyer, MD describes the restorative nature of the pouring rain.

Downpour

The rain falls overhead
  softly pattering
  soothing
  caressing

A melodious symphony of
nature
  beginning quietly
  gaining intensity
  until a steady, constant downpour.

A wondrous, private
concert
  experienced only by open ears
Music from the heavens so
precious
  I listen, enraptured
  cherishing the experience

Slowly tapering off
  until just the last lingering
drops
  gently land on the ground
  and then just a memory
  lingering in the air

The rain falls on my head
  mingling on my face
  with tears

easing my pain
my grief

Water provides sustenance,
an essential ingredient for
life,
It nourishes the earth
and my withered heart.

Healing my loss
Washing away my sorrow
Restoring my soul.

The colors of the sunrise remind Sharon Swinney of the beauty of her lost baby, Mary Beth, a pretty little red-haired child with blue eyes.

Memories At Sunrise

You should have seen the sunrise this morning.
The beautiful colours that herald the dawning.
As the night changed out of its dark nightdress,
Into a brand new day that was cool and fresh.

In the east, the sky was quite pale, almost white,
As the first rays pierced the darkness with light.
That pale first light had a lovely soft glow,
It reminded me of her skin with its soft, warm glow.

As the sun progressed and continued to grow,
The colours became stronger, pink, red, and mauve.
But it was the fiery red glow, in the cool morning air,
That danced and shimmered, just like her hair.

Then the sun came up and the show was over,
Except for the dew, which still clung on the clover.
Blue, pale blue, was the colour of the sky.
Just the same as her bright, smiling eyes.

Now every morning, when I rise,
I will go to the window and look to the skies.
For my memories are with me, my memories of Mary.
I have only to look to remember my baby.

SUPPORT

The pain of your grief is not usually visible to the outside world. For example, if you broke your leg and had to struggle around on crutches, people would probably help you in your struggle. With the emotional pain of grief, others are not alerted to your need for support. It's not their fault. Actually to them you probably look exactly the same as you did before your loss.

The only way to alert others of your inner pain is to tell them how you hurt. However, to speak out at a time when it's natural to turn inward is difficult. Now is the time to challenge that natural inclination of "keeping everything to yourself." When you suppress any strong feelings, you could become stuck in the grief process and held up in healing. That could lead to a variety of other emotional problems and even physical sicknesses.

One of the natural emotions of grief is anger. Some survivors have no trouble "working it off" or "running it off." Others may feel ashamed when they become angry. They may go to great lengths to avoid indicating that they're angry at all.

If you hesitate to show your anger in front of others, then simply go off by yourself and yell and scream until the anger is weakened. Discuss these feelings with someone close, join a support group and share those feelings. If your anger is intense and lingers, seek professional help. The worst thing you could do is to pretend that you have no anger.

A support group is a wonderful resource for most people. There's something about the grieving process—it eliminates barriers between people. Members of your group are not really strangers because you share the same journey. You can learn from a group about the steps of their journey, and gain comfort in your own. The benefits are enormous.

If at first you hesitate, just make a decision to try one or two meetings. If you don't find it worthwhile, you can quit. Usually a support group proves to be a new avenue for the very support you need.

Actually, all survivors have two kinds of support systems—the "natural" support system of family and friends and the "drafted" support system that you seek out. Sometimes it's impossible for our natural support system to meet all our emotional and practical needs.

Emotional support comes in the form of words of sympathy, companionship, sharing and advice, and counseling. You're not limited to family and friends for this support. But, if your family can't support you emotionally, you'll have to seek out others to connect with and talk to at this time. Practical support comes in the form of physical help, financial help, organization and planning assistance, and practical people who can keep you anchored in your decision making.

Here are some questions you might ask yourself:

1. Is the kind of support I'm currently receiving the sort of support I need and want? Why?
2. What kinds of support do I need?
3. What kinds of support do I least want?
4. What are my three greatest practical needs?
5. What are my three greatest emotional needs?

Here are some sources of support available to those who grieve:

1. Clergy
2. Close friends
3. Co-workers
4. Counseling/support groups
5. Counselor/therapist
6. Family physician
7. Family therapist
8. Home health care
9. Housekeeping
10. Immediate family
11. In-laws
12. Neighbors
13. School officials
14. Work supervisor
15. Teachers

Check off five sources of help that you might turn to and be ready to ask for help if necessary.

CHAPTER 20

TALKING

You're the only one who can tell your story—the story of your relationship with your loved one and the story of your loved one's death. Most of us who grieve memorize the story. We need to tell and retell that story. Each time you tell it you remove a small bit of hurt from inside you. You ease the wounds inside.

It's beneficial to tell the story of your loved one's death twice a day, three times a day, or more. If you still have the urge to tell it, that's what you must do.

Don't worry that others have heard it. They usually understand. Don't worry that your need to talk is excessive. By talking about a loved one you are giving testimony to their life. It gives significance to the strong influence they had in your life. In a way, repeating the story keeps the person alive. So your story is very important.

One woman felt both anger and love for her deceased husband: "I love him but WHY did he die when he knew we had a family to rear?" By identifying and expressing her anger as well as her love, this woman was taking steps to resolve her anger and restore inner peace. If she had suppressed her angry feelings, thinking they were wrong, she might have found herself loaded with deep-seated guilt and depression.

You may have to make the first move, unfair as it seems, to find good listeners from among your friends. Those who grieve with you cannot offer much comfort because they too need comfort and good listeners. Your friends may not offer a sympathetic ear, either because they may not know you need it or because they feel awkward. You can help them to help you. Ask for an open ear when you periodically need to express your feelings. Your friends can best offer comfort when they know about your pain.

By recounting special memories, you review your loved one's life and give value to the unique role they played in your life and the life of others. Sometimes we think that if we confide in someone else, if we tell the story of our loss, we are burdening the other person with our troubles or getting too personal. That's why it's valuable to choose a close friend—someone in whom you can continually confide. Perhaps someone who mourns the same person. If you appreciate and enjoy the company of the person, you can invite them into your life.

One good way to determine if a friendship is beneficial is to ask yourself how you feel after you meet. Is there a sense of release and relief from being with this person? If there is, perhaps you need to share your grief and pursue this nurturing friendship.

TIME

Life has a natural rhythm—sometimes time moves too quickly and sometimes too slowly. Your grief can slow time to a crawl—demanding much of you, day by day and minute by minute. The days and nights are longer now but in time they will assume their real length.

As your grief process moves on, you will find that time has accelerated too. You will reenter areas of your life you temporarily ignored. You'll become more involved in your work and family life again. When this happens, you may find that no longer is each day a test of agonizing endurance but a regular day, with a beginning, middle, and an end.

But how much time will it take to move beyond this grief? That is different for each of us. Just as life has its own rhythm, grief, which is a part of life, has its own time schedule. This time frame is controlled more by feelings and instinct than by any given rule. To try to force grief into a time frame or pattern will not work.

If people encourage you "not to dwell on it" and "to go on with life," they mean well but may not be considering what's in your heart. This is the time to look inside and let your needs and instincts guide you. Others may wish you to move on in your grief so that their lives become more normal. Perhaps, out of sympathy, they may simply wish to remove your pain. Remember that you can always respect the opinions of others but no one knows *you* as well as you know yourself. This is your grief. It belongs to you and only you!

Morning's Time

On that glorious day
Leaping clouds shouted—irrepressible
Against a teal-blue early spring sky.
Morning held an armful of joy in her apron
As she stood on the hillside, face to the sun.

~ ~

But Time raised his angry head—
Beating at her with a late blizzard wind,
Grabbing for her with gnarled branches.

~ ~

Morning
Squatted down on stubborn haunches,
Turning her back squarely to the whipping wind.

~ ~

Then I saw her tired feet slipping.

~ ~

Save me an hour!
I screamed, jumping to catch her;
Just one short hour
To keep in my hollow log, safe
Beneath a patchwork quilt of mosses,
So I can bring it out again
To sing to me of youthful love songs, and to
Waft delicate scents of spring blossoms over me,
On lonely frozen winter nights!

~ ~

But the wind raged higher, wilder—
And suddenly she lost her hold,
And blew away.

* * *

by Rosemary J. Gwaltney
www.crossingrivers.com

TRANSFORMATION

People will tell you that "time will take care of your grief." But just waiting for the passage of time after the loss of a loved one is not enough. The grief process represents a time of transformation.

There are some ways to pass time that are not healthy—becoming obsessed about activity, sleeping away our lives, dating twenty or thirty people, or sitting in front of the TV for the first year or two. We heal by feeling what we need to feel when we need to feel it.

We heal losses not because time passes but because of what we do with that time. It's helpful to spend time with others who are mourning to share the journey. It's not helpful to run from ourselves on the hopes that when we stop the grief-related feelings will disappear.

You can't remain passive and expect things to automatically get better. If nothing changes; nothing changes. The activity of grieving is recalling, feeling, sharing, and memorializing your loved one. Eventually a transition will take place where you will want to reach towards new life, not continuously reach backwards toward death. Knowing when to reach toward new life—new people, places, and things—is all part of this active transformation.

Storm

Last night we had a big thunderstorm,
This is what Mother Nature does when she mourns.
With thunder and lightening her anger is shown,
And the wind tears the trees, 'til they're all windblown.
The ice cold hail that comes crashing down,
Is broken from her heart and scattered on the ground.
The rain, her many teardrops falling,
Covers the ground to show she is mourning.

We had a storm like this the day Mary died.
Then another one came that night, while I cried.
But out of the storm new life begins.
The grass grows greener, the trees grow again.
Unfortunately there is no life without rain.

And sadly, we can't have a life without pain.
As hard as it is, we must weather life's storms,
We start our life anew, each time we mourn.

© by Sharon Swinney, Gleneagle, Australia

CHAPTER 21

UNIQUENESS OF GRIEF

Although each person's grief has individualistic characteristics, there are several factors that influence the length and depth of one's grief.

- *Age of The Deceased:* The younger the person the more difficult it is to mourn the death.
- *Cause of Death:* When loved one's know in advance that death is approaching they may experience much of their grief long before the actual death. Alternatively, the more sudden or violent the death, the longer one expects to grieve. Suddenness and violence add to the burden of grief.
- *Other Events in Our Life:* Sometimes one death follows another, or life's problems make it necessary to put grief on hold. The need to mourn is still there and will emerge at a later date.
- *Support Systems:* The more support you have the quicker your recovery is likely to be, but you will still need time to reflect on your loss, mourn fully, and become comfortable with the loss.
- *Community Resources:* It will help if you have access to the library or the local bookstore for appropriate reading. Affiliation with a church or community group can help you find a support group. Living near an area that generally provides a variety of resources is helpful.
- *Your Own Coping Skills:* When you understand your own pattern of coping skills, you can draw on this knowledge. In looking back to other times of crisis, you might examine how you handled other

situations. What coping skills were positive? What ones were not? Refining your own set of skills can help shorten your grief.

- *Gender Differences:* There seems to be gender differences, dominated by the popular culture, in the expression of grief. Generally, women are allowed to express their emotions while men, traditionally, have been held back. Although recent years have seen changes in this thinking, some biases still exist. Both genders need to be allowed free expression of grief.

Your grief is as unique as you are! Honor that uniqueness. There is no standard recipe that can neatly be applied to every situation. Expect to react in ways that are different from everyone else.

UNFINISHED BUSINESS

Unfinished business can hamper the progression of your grief. If your relationship had any difficulties that were not responded to—such as arguments not settled, situations of mental, physical, sexual or emotional abuse not properly terminated, or even questions not asked, or love unspoken—there may be unfinished business.

When you can't find resolution, you may feel restless, unable to grieve the way you'd like to. You may see others moving along in their grief and wonder why you seem so stuck. To further complicate the issue, others may lose patience with what is happening to you and withdraw their support. Their withdrawal will only cause further pain and more unfinished business.

Therefore, it's very important that we resolve the unfinished business with the deceased, find some resolution—either by your own grief work or with the help of a therapist. Sometimes a qualified professional is needed because the situation may be too complex for us to handle. Usually unfinished business carries with it deep emotional responses that we don't understand.

Here are some things that you might do to start:

1. Figure out exactly what the unfinished business is by listing everything that was unresolved when the death occurred.
2. Look at your list and think about what you could do to get some relief and resolve this issue. Some ways that others have used are writing a letter, making an audio-tape that addresses the issue, creating a collage to symbolize the issue. These activities will allow the survivor expression of every detail of the problem.
3. Determine what method will work for you and write the letter or make the audio-tape or collage. Then, in time you might decide

what to do with these things. Some people burn the letter and spread the ashes at the gravesite. Some people share the audiotape or collage with a trusted friend or therapist.

4. If you hesitate to create anything material that might be found or misunderstood, then you may speak directly about the subject using the picture of the deceased placed in a chair in front of you. Say all you need to say—yell, scream, cry—apologize if that is appropriate.

Since unresolved issues will hold you back in your grieving, it's best not to dismiss them and do nothing. Thinking they will just go away won't work. Usually without resolution these issues reoccur, remaining "unresolved" future problems.

Expressing regrets is part of the unfinished business of grief. Addressing unfinished business doesn't necessarily require endless hours of soul searching. Sometimes it requires no more than voicing regret for things done or left undone.

REGRETS:

1. I wish I'd said ______________________________
2. I wish you'd said______________________________
3. I wish I had ______________________________
4. I wish I hadn't______________________________
5. I wish you had______________________________
6. I wish you hadn't ______________________________
7. I wish I could change______________________________
8. I'm sorry for ______________________________
9. I wish ______________________________
10. I wish ______________________________

Here are some helpful ideas to think about once you have brought to light your regrets. Are there things you can do that can solve any of your unresolved regrets? Are there actions that you can take in your life which might help you to feel better about these regrets? Are there some problem situations in your present relationships—things unsaid or undone—that you need to correct before they become unresolved regrets at a later time?

UNANTICIPATED TEARS

Feelings may pour forth at unexpected times even when there doesn't seem to be an outside source to provoke them. You might begin to cry in the supermarket, while driving home from work, or eating out in a restaurant. It can happen so fast that you are at a loss to explain what you are crying about.

When my father died, I was only fourteen and had particular difficulty with unanticipated tears. Perhaps it was my general emotional state at that young age but I remember my emotions were always right on the edge. I couldn't seem to control the tears. A sudden thought about the way that my father looked as he was dying could bring tears. Other times I would cry when someone mentioned his or her father. Sometimes it happened right in the classroom. There was no anticipating it and there was no sense to it. I never knew when I might start crying.

Somehow I thought I needed to explain myself to others when the tears started. But there was no way to explain how deep my sadness was. So I usually removed myself from the situation and calmed myself down by being alone.

Sometimes your grief can catch up with you and overwhelm you—even years after the death. A middle aged woman whose father died when she was six burst into tears when she was attending a party. A band had just begun to play. Somehow this woman, in remembering that her father had been a musician, connected what was happening to a very early memory of her father when he was on stage playing in a band. There was something about one of the men and the way he was smiling and tapping his foot. Seeing this man made her feel the loss and she burst into tears.

With any deep sorrow, there can be repeated occasional incidences of spontaneous crying throughout your life. They probably will be less frequent after the first year or two; however, they can still happen anytime.

Expressed grief is always beneficial. Unexpressed grief usually manifests itself in some other form—sleeplessness, heart palpitations, irregular breathing, weight loss, or other physical ailments.

You might look at these unanticipated tears, not as a burden, but as gifts that help you release the "uncried" tears that are the residue of your grief process. Don't be alarmed, just let it happen and be grateful for the release. You will never totally recover from this loss, let it be a part of you.

CORN SILK SORROW

Sorrow is like long, silken
corn flax, that lies within the web
of the husk.

It is waiting there for the corn husker!

You think you can get by it,
not notice it, make it go away,
but it is there.

Clinging to everything, creating memory
moments that hang on. Yes!
Sorrow is like corn silk.

CHAPTER 22

VULNERABILITY

Most people feel vulnerable after the death of a loved one. Yet, even though we know we're suffering we're tempted to shut ourselves off from the sources of help. We might say we are doing fine and want to be left alone. On the inside we might feel frightened, confused, or lonely.

Knowing we are hurting, yet closing ourselves off from all help, can become a self-punishment if carried to the extreme. If only we can admit how we feel, others will be able to help. No one is always capable, strong, logical, or patient.

When you lose someone close in an accidental death, you may feel particularly vulnerable. I remember that kind of vulnerability when my brother was killed in a plane crash. Michael was close to me, just a year and a half younger than me. His death was unexpected and seemed untimely since we were both in our early thirties.

When the accident happened, the Associated Press Wire Service picked up the story, printing sensational pictures of the actual accident along with a photo of my brother only minutes before his death. That kind of exposure only served to increase my sense of vulnerability.

I remember being inordinately, instinctively, afraid after the accident. Because I had experienced an unexpected, personal trauma, I feared for myself and those around me. This fear dominated my behavior and influenced my attitude. It was difficult to see planes, and especially to hear them.

Ironically, seven days after the death of my brother my two-year-old son was hit by a car in front of my house. Luckily, the accident only caused a superficial head wound and he survived. But the sight of the accident stunned me. When I saw the car hit him, I ran out screaming "Oh, no, God, not again." Instinctively, I was aware I couldn't bear another loss.

I was terrified on the trip into the hospital and in the days after that second accident. My young son suffered from the same sense of fear and vulnerability, and my inability to calm him kept us both traumatized for months. In time the fear dissipated and we both felt less vulnerable.

Death comes in many forms—we lose a parent, a good friend, a beloved grandmother. We lose a loved one in the violence of murder, terrorism, war, or in the despair of suicide. All of these deaths carry their own kind of grief and the circumstances of the loss may affect the level of vulnerability. Deaths that occur suddenly or accidentally can cause a deeper trauma.

Trauma makes us feel vulnerable. Actually, any unexpected occurrence, even the most mundane, can unnerve us. You back into a car in a parking lot. You get back on the road wondering what will happen next. There seems to be danger everywhere.

The truth is, accidents happen when we are most vulnerable. So it's best not to expect too much of yourself when you're in the throes of grief. Do what's required of you, but don't take on too much until you're ready. Ask yourself, is this trip necessary at this time; can I put off making this decision today; can I postpone this activity for tomorrow? Do only what you know you can handle!

Certain thoughts and attitudes might be the result of your vulnerable state. If you lose a spouse or parent you might:

1. Think of death more frequently.
2. Feel sick all the time.
3. Feel a sense of financial insecurity.
4. Feel insecure about the future.
5. Have a sense of impending doom.

These thoughts may not be rooted in fact but come from your increased vulnerability at this time. In time they should subside.

If you think you are weak, and find yourself being "too hard on yourself" for this vulnerable state, work on self-acceptance. Ask yourself: Am I treating myself better or worse than I would treat a friend? Then, befriend yourself! Work on your health—physical and emotional. Make time for yourself today. Enhance your social life and physical environment. Just be good to yourself!

CHAPTER 23

W

WITHDRAWAL

You may feel as if you want to hide forever but the circumstances of life, job, relationships, and other commitments make it necessary to leave the safety of your home. There are times you may wish you could stay inside rather than going back to work, taking care of the kids, attending to the errands, or looking after the needs of others.

Going out for the first time is the most difficult. After that, subsequent trips will be easier. Once you have stepped outside and closed the door behind you, you will have made the hardest part of the journey.

The very nature of grief itself is an antisocial state. Most survivors tend to avoid gatherings. There may be a feeling of not wanting to have people see us. We may not want to hide our sad feelings. Conversation may seem inane. It's hard to concentrate on things that don't interest us at all.

You may get impatient with your anti-social feelings and wish you could change. Remember it's OK to pull away into a place of privacy to help resolve the loss. This feeling of withdrawal may last as much as a year. It's only when the grieving results in complete withdrawal—or prolonged withdrawal—that we need to worry. In that case it might be necessary to get professional help.

You have a right to withdraw now without making excuses or feeling guilty. Wait until you feel more comfortable being around other people, until you have more energy, until you don't feel so vulnerable. Then the time will come to test the waters in the world outside.

You may come to venture out for a short time and take part in some activity you once enjoyed. Have dinner with a friend. See a movie. Attend a sports event. Visit the home of friends. Attend a lecture or concert. Or just meet a friend for coffee. Even though it may seem easier to just remain withdrawn, it's crucial for your emotional health to venture out. Start with something very simple. Schedule it by writing it into your calendar and committing to it.

That Perilous Lip

Behind the rolling purple clouds
Gleams sunlight's brilliant glow;
Beneath the bitter snow
The crocus bulbs unfold and grow;
And through these dark gray skies behold
A bending neon bow.

~ ~ ~

Despite the shout of thunderclaps
Oh may this weight of living's grief
Rest lightly on my brow;
Oh may I now
Think long of him—the one I miss—
Come gently to the precipice
But yet not fall.
I wish to feel it all,
Still never tip
Beyond that perilous lip.

by Rosemary J. Gwaltney
www.crossingrivers.com

WISDOM

Grief may bring to us a "costly wisdom." It's a wisdom we usually don't seek out. Coming through a great sorrow can make us stronger and teach us what is really important. Eleanor Roosevelt once said, "You gain strength, courage and confidence by every experience in which you really stop to look fear in the face. You are able to say to yourself, 'I have lived through this horror. I can take the next thing that comes along.' You must do the thing you think you cannot do."

Immediately after thousands of Americans were killed in the horrible destruction of the World Trade Twin Towers in New York City, the country seemed to become wiser. We began to see the real danger of terrorists' threats; we were shaken from our cocoon of complacency.

Now we were ready to take strenuous measures to protect our people from outside forces. In a horribly painful way, we had gained a certain national wisdom.

Ironically, after the September 11 tragedy at the Twin Towers, our nation gained a better sense of who we are and what we most want in life. Everywhere people displayed their patriotism by honoring the American flag. Unanimously, people declared "I am proud to be an American." Obviously, the terrorists' aim was to destroy America, but instead our country became stronger in its adversity.

A national grief set in motion the desire of many to reshape their lives in more heroic terms. Firemen, policemen and policewomen, volunteers, military men and women worked tirelessly to find the dead and clear the debris, ordinary citizens gave their goods, their time, and money to help the victims. As survivors of a crisis, a new power—a new wisdom—emerged because of the choices people made during those horrific moments of sorrow.

This poem was written on September 16, 2001 by Susan Godman Rager in honor and in memory of those lost September 11, 2001.

Omega

Letters overflowing inboxes
Busy conversations
Coffee perking
Elevators climbing
Plants watered
It is the day beginning
on Tuesday
the last Tuesday
Empty tables
at Windows on the World
waiting for
glittering chats and
gleaming silver
The world waiting for trade
for the exchange of
who owns what and where
and for who will win and who will
lose
And the morning drifted by
as mornings do
with nothing outstanding
nothing understanding
that this is all
the mornings there would be

A shudder, a powerful pull
a push, a gust, a split
an opening into sky and flame
and smoke beyond all night

and dust beyond all deserts
and a clutching of the building
on itself
as it tried within its bones
to stand
And its heart was melting
and souls were flying
And a sound
of twin pain
was to its side
another scrape of
metal on metal and glass
on glass and the whoosh
of air and fuel and flame
and the pall of smoke
that ate the breath
of everything that
moved

Side by side
they stood
two terrible wounds
pulling them apart
the steel without gleaming
the steel within melting
their people
all their dear and lovely people
that they knew
that they harbored
every day every Tuesday
every floor, every suite
all of this falling slowly
surely down in a
measured sure death

and suddenly one
without the ability to stand
longer
fell
and in its falling
lasted lifetimes
centuries of hopes

sighs dreams
falling with pictures
with eyeglasses
with outboxes whose papers
flew
far beyond their
intended destinations
into forever
And the other
the one who waited
still stood for awhile
and at last let go
nothing to do but fall
nowhere to go but where
the other had gone
no reason to stay
the lonely sky without its twin
too much
too long
too alone
And as it fell
and all within
part of its terrible death
there were years in its falling
there were centuries of conversations
and eons of memories
and civilizations of laughter and tears
and birthdays and life celebrations
and first days and last days
and the middle that we know
as life and as it fell on itself

bone by bone
of its very existence
becoming dust
the sky wrenched and twisted
and pulled away
from the sound
the awful
tearing
sound
and tried to withdraw
from the smoke
that was the life breath
of the building
and of its children
those it harbored

every day
and the silence became unattainable
any more
for those watching
hearing
mouths open
the silence only belonged
to those
within
whose last desperate day
was that day
as they left
the highest place
they had ever been
to go to
the truly
highest place
angels
and wings of angels
and feathers
going up
into
the clear blue sky

far above the smoke
far beyond the
terrible groan and roar
far into where we believe heaven is,
far into where we believe
all hands were awake, alert
and pulling them upwards
fast
out of the pain
out of the grief
and into the music
of peace.

CHAPTER 24

XMAS: CHRISTMAS AND HOLIDAYS

Holidays! How do you ignore them when they are all so commercialized? It's almost impossible. So even though you may not wish to be reminded of days like Mother's Day, Father's Day, or Valentine's Day, there they are—everywhere—in the store windows, in newspaper ads, and on TV. There's no escape, so you might as well meet the holidays head on and make plans for them.

Christmas is the most celebrated holiday of the year in this country. It will surround you—coming at you from all sides. There's the inevitable gift giving and special family event. All of these things can become reminders of your loss.

Little Lost Face

The children's Christmas is simple and bright
They sing the music, they laugh in the light
Sparkling colors are a magical spell
Their instant joy flows bubbling and well.

~ ~ ~

But round that tree I see a space
Beside the table an empty place
A voice is missing, a form of grace
The sweetness of a little lost face.

~ ~ ~

A vacuum was left by the child who's gone
Though all seems right, something's terribly wrong
I'd give up my Christmas and gaity fine
To clasp that small hand again in mine.

www.crossingrivers.com

Here are some ideas that may make your holidays more bearable.

1. Think out carefully how much of this holiday you can handle. Writing out cards may prove to be too much, so don't do it this year. Or writing cards may be your opportunity to let others know of your loss. It's up to you. If decorating seems too much, cut back this year. Then, let it go.

2. You may not want to shop in stores this year because you keep thinking of the things you would have gotten for your loved one this year. Find other ways to gather your gifts—Internet shopping, catalogs, or simply money gifts.

3. Once you have decided what your place is in this holiday season, discuss it with you family and friends. Small children usually have to be accommodated because they don't understand grief. Jacqueline Kennedy, who was known to be a dedicated mother, decided to have John Kennedy Jr's birthday party as planned even though she had just witnessed the brutal murder of her husband. Sometimes for the sake of children you do what is necessary even though it's difficult. Do what you need to do, but do only what you are capable of.

4. You may decide to do something totally different, especially in the first year after your loss, so that you don't run into constant reminders. You may decide to keep busy and work on the holiday. Be careful that you don't feel deprived if you make this choice. You may decide to serve dinner to the homeless on Christmas Day. Usually thinking of someone else helps get your mind off your sorrow. You may decide to attend a church service or a concert. Try to find one that you never attended before. Doing something different, or something to help others, can get you through the holidays.

5. If you have a support group, they might schedule a meeting close to the holidays. Share your pain and it will lessen.

Other Religious and Secular Holidays

Christmas isn't the only celebrated day. There are other religious holidays like Easter, the Passover, Yom Kippur, Thanksgiving, Hanukkah, and Ramadan. And the secular holidays like Valentine's Day, Mother's Day, or Father's Day. All can be troublesome.

Think about which holidays have meant the most to you. Be prepared by having a plan for that day. Start a brand new tradition. Share your turkey with someone who might be alone for Thanksgiving or Christmas. Remember a child or someone special on Valentine's Day with a gift you have made or a card.

Special Personal Occasions

Part of the grief process is successfully getting through special occasions without your loved one. There are the inevitable weddings, funerals, anniversaries, and birthday parties. All can be powerfully painful!

The keys to survival are preparation and awareness. First, you need to prepare for any special occasion that might trouble you. Tell a friend or family member that you might need some support. Be aware and don't underestimate the power of these special occasions. Special days usually evoke memories.

Particularly difficult times might be wedding anniversaries and the first anniversary of the death of your loved one. Make plans for what you need to do that day. You might wish to be alone, to visit the cemetery, to write a special note to your loved one. Prepare your friends and family by telling them you will need help or letting them know that you wish to be left alone. In time these days will become less painful.

CHAPTER 25

YEARNINGS

When we lose a key person in our life—a parent, spouse, grandparent, or mentor—there's usually a sense of discontinuity. A daughter may long for her mother, wishing her mother could see how her life has turned out, wishing her mother could participate in important life events. We usually miss our parents when things are going well and we want to share our joy or when things are going badly and we desperately need nurturing.

There may be a longing that occurs in the course of normal everyday living when you find you can't contact your loved one and communicate with them. No longer can you pick up the phone and call, stop by and see them, or go to some special place you always went to. You long to do these simple things.

You long to have your loved one with you to share a special meal, or just take a walk. You may wish they could see the children growing up. The yearning for the companionship of your loved one can be particularly acute if you shared a deep and meaningful relationship.

No one is an island! All of us need to have the advice and loving support of someone. Most of the time a healthy person can handle his or her own emotional crises. But on certain occasions we all need to make contact with some special person who calms us, who brings us back to reason, and who has always been there for us. When we are grieving and particularly vulnerable, we may long to have that connection again.

When I detect that sense of longing for continuity, I find it helpful to revisit the grave of my mother, who is a source of strength to me, and mentally check in with her. In the first few years after her death I really missed our talks. My visits to her grave were more frequent then.

Today, I still visit but I have found others who fill in my life with a mother's love. It takes time to build meaningful bonds with others. Sometimes a grown child or long lost friends or relatives can become a source of continuity in your life. Being open to the possibility of love is most important after a loss. There are many avenues of connection.

CHAPTER 26

Z

ZEST

Many times when we meet death face to face we become a changed person. Now, we are asked to survive the loss of our loved one but also we have been reminded about the brevity of life and the certainty of our own death. Life's short span has been underscored because usually we don't expect death.

Then come the questions: "What am I going to do with the rest of my life? Will I live it with fervor? Will I appreciate every day? Will I adopt a new zest for life in the precious time I have to live?"

The grief experience can give this special gift of conviction—that our life is a time to be lived fully, regardless of the number of years we have. Now we can reinvest our energies, make our plans, carry out those plans, explore, help, create, learn, grow, and delight in all that is around us. With this new zest for life we can become more alive to life itself.

Sometimes it's so simple! I remember when my friend David died an early death. Unfortunately, he lived a life that invited death because he never really beat his addiction to alcohol. His end was sudden, tragic, yet not unexpected. There were only a few friends at the gravesite and it was over in a moment.

As I was leaving the cemetery, I felt a sense of emptiness at a lifetime wasted. Then, I noticed a bluebird nearby which reminded me that David always appreciated beautiful things. Once he gave me a beautiful silk scarf of vivid hues—blues, pinks, and fuchsia colors. Somehow, the blue color of the bird, there amidst the bleakness of death, reminded me to become more aware of the colors of life and to live my life more vibrantly. Every time I see a bluebird, I find strength and solace in its color and renew the powerful lesson of that day.

After the initial months of early grief we become survivors. Then as survivors, we have a choice. We can make a decision to just get through life day by day or we can learn to renew our commitment to life. We can curse our fate because things are difficult or we can reenter the world knowing that now we have a reverence for things that were perhaps formerly taken for granted—like the color of a bluebird.

The grief process is so complex that it covers the entire alphabet. We have gone from A to Z trying to understand grief. Only to conclude that grief is not to be understood, just experienced.

The brother of a firefighter killed as he was trying to save others told me, "I hope I never stop grieving. I hope it never ends even though I am hurting every day. Even though I am reminded every day, I hope the hurt never ends because it lets me know how meaningful my brother's life really was."

The final question is always, "What knowledge can I take from the grief experience?" Then, "How can that knowledge make my life more meaningful?" It may take some time to find the answers to these questions but they are there within us.

References

Borysenko, Joan, *Guilt is the Teacher, Love is the Lesson: A Book to Heal Your Heart and Soul,* Warner Books, New York, 1990.

Brunton, Paul, quote from *The Quotable Soul: Inspiring Quotations Crossing Time and Culture,* John Wiley & Sons, Inc., New York, 1994.

Chaucer, Geoffrey, *The Canterbury Tales,* K. Hieatt and C. Hieatt (eds.), Bantam Classics, New York, 1982.

Dickinson, Emily, *The Complete Poems of Emily Dickinson,* Little, Brown, Boston, 1924.

Euripedes, *Heracles,* 422 B.C., W. Arrowsmith (trans.), quote from *The International Thesaurus of Quotations,* R. T. Tripp (compiler), Harper and Row, New York, 1970.

Hayer, Marly, Light in the Darkness, *Caring Concepts Newsletter,* The Centering Corporation, Omaha, Nebraska, 1991.

Jacobsen, Joan, One Tulip, *Caring Concepts Newsletter,* The Centering Corporation, Omaha, Nebraska, 1992.

Laing, Ronald David, The Tie and The Cut Off, *The Voice of Experience,* Pantheon Books, New York, 1982..

Mendel, Stephanie, *March, before Spring,* O'Brien & Whitaker, Oakland, California, 1999.

Sarton, May, *Shadow of a Man,* W. W. Norton, New York, 1950.

Simpson, Michael A., *The Facts of Death,* Prentice-Hall, Englewood Cliffs, New Jersey, 1979.

Straudacher, Carol, *A Time to Grieve, Meditations for Healing After the Death of a Loved One,* HarperCollins Publishers, New York, 1994.

Swinney, Sharon, *From the Heart, A Mother's Journey Through Grief,* SANDS (QLD) Inc., Queensland, Australia, 1996.

Williamson, Marianne, The Power of Positive Thinking, *The Oprah Magazine, 1*:5, November 2000.

Wolfelt, Alan D., Dispelling 5 Common Myths About Grief, *Thanatos,* Fall 1989.

Additional Book Sources

Bennett, Amanda and Foley, Terrence B. *In memoriam: A Practical Guide to Planning a Memorial Service.* New York: Simon and Schuster, 1997.

Caplan, Sandi and Lang, Gordon. *Grief's Courageous Journey: A Workbook.* Oakland, California: New Harbinger Publications, Inc., 1995.

Dotterweich, Kass P. *Grieving as a Woman: Moving Through Life's Many Losses.* St. Meinrad, Indiana: Abbey Press, 1998.

Firzgerald, Helen. *The Mourning Book: The Most Comprehensive Resource Offering Practical and Compassionate Advice on Coping with All Aspects of Death and Dying.* New York: Simon and Schuster, 1994.

Guest, Anthony, *A Little Book of Comfort: An Anthology of Grief and Love.* London. England: Marshall Pickering, 1995.

Hickman, Martha Whitmore. *Healing After Loss: Daily Meditations for Working Through Grief.* New York: Avon Books, 1994.

Jensen, Amy Hillyard. *Healing Grief.* Redmond, Washington: Medic Publishing Company, 1980.

Klass, Dennis, Silverman, Phyllis R., and Nickman, Steven L. (editors). *Continuing Bonds: New Understandings of Grief.* Philadelphia, Pennsylvania: Taylor and Francis, 1996.

Manning, Doug. *Don't Take My Grief Away: What to Do When You Lose a Loved One.* New York: HarperCollins Publishers, 1984.

Moffat, Mary Jane (editor). *In the Midst of Winter: Selections from Literature of Mourning.* New York: Vintage Books, 1982.

Rich, Phil. *The Healing Journey Through Grief: Your Journal for Reflection and Recovery.* New York: John Wiley & Sons, Inc., 1999.

Rosof, Barbara D. *The Worst Loss: How Families Heal from the Death of a Child.* New York: Henry Holt and Company, 1994.

Swinney, Sharon. *From the Heart: A Mother's Journey Through Grief.* Queensland, Australia: SANDS (Qld) Inc., 1996.

Shaw, Eva. *What To Do When a Loved One Dies: A Practical and Compassionate Guide to Dealing with Death on Life's Terms.* Irvine, California: Dickens Press, 1994.

Straudacher, Carol. *Beyond Grief: A Guide for Recovering from the Death of a Loved One.* Oakland, California: New Harbinger Publications, Inc., 1987.
Straudacher, Carol. *A Time to Grieve: Meditations for Healing After the Death of a Loved One.* New York: HarperCollins Publishers, 1994.

Contributors

Judy Burnette-Martin

Judy was born and grew up in Tennessee. She said, "Like every young child I dreamed of a perfect world where everything was beautiful. As I grew older, I realized pain visits us all in some form or other. My brother was killed when I was a freshman in high school and I wrote my first poem then. Eight years later my dad died suddenly with a heart attack just weeks before my first child was born."

"Over the course of years pain has visited me on a regular basis. Yet, I have learned that he is only a visitor and cannot stay in my life always. I must deal with his entrance and still live my life to the fullest. May the poems I have written in some way touch your life and help your heart to mend." More of Judy's work can be found at netpoets.com under Judy Burnette.

Caring Concepts/Centering Corporation

(Permission to reprint *Light in the Darkness* by Marly Hayer; *One Tulip* by Joan Jacobsen; and *Please See Me through My Tears* by Kelly Osmont.)

Caring Concepts is the newsletter from Centering Corporation, North America's oldest and largest bereavement resource center. Since 1976, Centering Corporation has published over 150 books on grief (many for children), has provided workshops and conferences, and serves as a clearinghouse for other bereavement publishers.

Centering Corporation, 7230 Maple St., Box 4600, Omaha NE 68104. Ph: 402-553-1200, Fax: 402-553-0507, e-mail: jl200@aol.com, Web site: www.centering.org.

Steve Channing

In 1987 Steven Channing lost his fourteen-year-old daughter, Kimberly Susanne Channing—April 15, 1973–February 23, 1987. He is a former member of the Winnipeg Peer Counseling Service, Winnipeg, Canada. Steven started up several Survivor's of Suicide Groups after his daughter's death. He credits the love, guidance, and understanding of the group in helping him through a difficult period.

Steve says, "the more I reach out to others, the softer and firmer her memory comes back to me." Steve's poem can be found on some Web sites of "The Compassionate Friends," an organization that helps survivors who have lost children. E-mail address inacoma@shaw.ca.

Susan Dane

Susan Dane was originally trained in classical piano, including studies at the Conservatoire de Paris in France. She later went on to study poetry with Glover Davis, a student of Philip Levine. *GOOD-BYE TO WHITE KNIGHTS and Other Moving Vehicles,* her first volume, traces her deeply personal journey from disillusionment and despair as a young woman into a world where Spirit is Art, and life the journey of the artist.

Susan has had an active career in personal counseling and spiritual healing for nearly 20 years. She speaks French, Spanish, and Portuguese, and has given workshops on spirituality throughout the United States and Europe. She has also been interviewed on world-wide radio and been a frequent contributor to the *Christian Science Monitor.*

Susan has just completed her first book, *WHEN ALL SYSTEMS FAIL: Spiritual Answers Beyond Self-Help.* She currently divides her time between New York, where her son, Preston, is an actor, and the south of France, where her two Chihuahuas, Jo-Jo and Julio, enjoy chasing pigeons on the beach. Susan can be reached through her Web site [www.susandane.com] which includes seminar information, poetry, and articles on "Genuine Spirituality—Free From all Systems."

Kirsti A. Dyer, MD, MS, FAAETS, BCETS, BCBT, NCBF

Dr. Dyer is a physician with a special interest in grief and loss issues. Since finishing her internal medicine training, she has pursued her own post-graduate Fellowship training in grief, loss, bereavement, and traumatic stress. She has completed post-graduate education in loss, grief, bereavement, end-of-life care, medical art therapy, poetry therapy, critical incident stress debriefing, trauma, and post-traumatic stress disorder. Dr. Dyer is a Fellow with the American Academy of Experts in Traumatic Stress (FAAETS), board certified in bereavement trauma (BCBT) and traumatic stress (BCTS). She is one of the few internists to become a Nationally Certified Bereavement Facilitator (NCBF) from the American Academy of Bereavement.

Her interest in grief and in the Medical Internet culminated in the creation of Journey of Hearts™, www.journeyofhearts.org, a non-profit Web site devoted to the issues of grief and loss. The site provides medical, non-medical information, and grief aid to the American and international Internet communities. Dr. Dyer has presented scientific papers about Journey of Hearts™ at a variety of international conferences in London (England), Heidelberg (Germany), Victoria (Canada), and Maui (Hawaii). She has lectured for Kaiser Permanente, U.C. Berkeley Extension, California Maritime Academy, and the American Medical Student's Association.

Dr. Dyer has shared poems with her patients as a way of connecting with them. Many of her poems are included as resources on Journey of Hearts™. People have used her poems in funeral services, published as memorials in papers, sent as e-mail condolences, and published in grief resources and books.

Since having her first daughter in March 2000, she practices medicine part-time. She expects her second daughter in the spring 2002. Most of her time is devoted to being a full-time mother. The remaining time is spent maintaining Journey of Hearts,™, educating, teaching, and writing on grief and loss.

Rosemary J. Gwaltney

When I was a child, my loving mother breathed the magical fire of language into my young mind. It developed into a passion which has never waned. Many times in my life, I have known grief. And being able to put my sorrow into words has been a comfort. While growing up, though extremely monetarily poor, I remained virtually unaware of it, we lived so far from society. I enjoyed a rich heritage of love, language, and heartfelt faith throughout my extended family.

Though many of my babies were lost to miscarriage, two living children were born to me. After that, my entire adulthood was spent adopting, raising, and loving children with handicaps: mental, physical, or both. This has been the source of both superb happiness, and overwhelming grief. Seven children over the thirty-one years have died of their severe disabilities. Sixteen children are living today, mostly grown, and are dearly treasured.

Each of my children I loved passionately, and always will. I know we will all be reunited again for all of eternity in Heaven. I spent evenings through all the years, writing about every one of my beloved children. I'm currently working on a book, *Gold Leaves In Winter,* which tells these very special children's tender stories. Poems about my children can be found on: "Coming Through the Fire," my site for bereaved people: www.angelfire.com/zine/bereaved/

I'm the survivor of an extraordinary, multifaceted life. But I'm a strong believer in a supreme and loving God. He created me to be a somewhat reclusive dreamer, a dancer to different music, intensely nurturing, and very individualistic. He gave His son Jesus, Who is my personal Saviour, and He gave me the strength to survive the anguish this life has held.

Over the years, I've had many articles of non-fiction published in magazines, including: "Sharing Our Caring," "The Exceptional Parent," "Home Education," "Growing Without Schooling," "Nursing the Dying Child," "Natthan," "Broken Hearts, Living Hope," and "Gentle Spirit." Also published was my chapter in the book "Adopting Children With Special Needs: A Sequel."

I'm the happy and grateful wife of the wonderful man I've loved since eleven years old, and who is my main inspiration, being my fascinating companion in writing. Dale and I are enjoying our mature years writing together. A compilation of some of our writing is presented on www.crossingrivers.com.

Michael MacCarthy

Mr. MacCarthy is an award-winning author, publisher, and ghostwriter. During recent years, he has collaborated, edited, or "book-doctored" dozens of projects. Most recently, he worked as "book-doctor" for Janice MacDonald who sold a three-book deal to Harlequin: *The Doctor Delivers—May 2002; The Man on the Cliffs*—August 2002; and *Family Matters*—No pub date yet.

Another novel, *The Celestial Bar: A Spiritual Journey* by Tom Youngholm (ghostwritten by MacCarthy), was originally self-published and later sold at auction to Delacorte Press for a six-figure advance. A nonfiction book, *Fiber Optics and the Telecommunications Explosion* by Norma Thorsen (Simon & Schuster, Prentice Hall Division) landed in bookshelves shortly before Christmas 1997. Another nonfiction book, *Business Buyer's Kit* by Michael Smorenburg (Career Press), went to bookstores in April 1998. Another novel, *From Amigos to Friends* by Pelayo "Pete" Garcia (Arte Público, Piñata Books Division), arrived in bookstores in the late spring of 1999.

Mr. MacCarthy is also the editor and publisher of *San Diego Writers' Monthly,* the county's only monthly literary magazine. It has won numerous awards from The Society of Professional Journalists and the San Diego Press Club for excellence in writing, editing, and graphic arts.

Mike has taught writing to adults and chaired a weekly "Read and Critique"; he currently teaches Creative Writing at a private high school. He often speaks about writing as a career at colleges, universities, and education associations throughout southern California. He also is a frequent guest speaker at writers' conferences and before writers' groups throughout the Southwest.

To contact Mr. MacCarthy, write or call care of:

San Diego Writers' Monthly
3910 Chapman Street
San Diego, CA 92110
(619) 226-0896
e-mail: mcarthy@sandiego-online.com

Stephanie Mendel

Stephanie Mendel is the author of *March, before Spring,* a book of poetry about her husband's death and her grief. The book has been used by hospice in groups dealing with the loss of a spouse. Joan Monheit, LCSW says, "Her evocative poems provide solace and support, as well as a reminder that others too have survived the painful loss of a spouse."

She and her late husband met in Ann Arbor, Michigan in the fifties, were married for thirty-five years, living mainly in the San Francisco Bay area. They have two sons and two grandsons. Stephanie teaches writing, and her work has appeared in many literary journals as well as *The Hospice of Marin News, The Stanford University Hospital Medical Staff Update, The Western Journal of Medicine,* and *The Saturday Evening Post.* The Web site for her book is http://www.themendels.org/widows/.

Martie Odell-Ingebretsen

Martie Odell-Ingebretsen has been writing poetry for nearly 30 years. She has been published in a number of books and magazines, including *Who's Who in Poetry in American Colleges and Universities.* She has also written numerous short stories and is at work on two novels. She posts many of her poems on a Web site, Passions in Poetry, where she is a moderator http://piptalk.com/.

Martie has always found that poetry has helped her express the way she feels about life. When her daughter, Michelle, died at the age of eight, writing poetry was a healing tool. Her poetry and photos of her daughter can be found at a Web site for grief, "Coming Through the Fire" by Rosemary and Dale Gwaltney. The URL to Michelle's room is http://www.angelfire.com/zine/bereaved/michelleopen.html

Martie lives in southern California where she and her husband own a flower shop. Martie can be reached at Martiword@hotmail.com

Kelly Osmont

Kelly Osmont, MSW, is a therapist in private practice in Portland. She is also a speaker and author. After her only child's death, a 19-year-old son, Aaron, she authored one book and two booklets. They are: *Parting Is Not Goodbye,* and the booklets are *More Than Surviving . . . Caring for Yourself While You Grieve* and *What Can I Say? How to Help Someone Who is Grieving: A Guide.* All are available through Centering Corp, Inc. in Omaha, Nebraska.

Susan Rager

Susan Godman Rager received her Juris Doctor degree from the T. C. Williams School of Law at the University of Richmond, Virginia. Undergraduate studies (English, honors) were completed at Virginia Commonwealth University in Richmond. She is a member of the bar in the Commonwealth of Virginia, the State of Maryland, and the District of Columbia, and a majority of her law practice centers on criminal defense. Her office is located in Historic Downtown Coles Point, Westmoreland County, in the historic Northern Neck of Virginia.

Writing, photography, and Web site design and management are current hobbies. The Northern Neck of Virginia Law Page at http://www.ragerlaw.com, which is a mix of personal and business presentations, has been updated weekly since the site began in November 1997. Her e-mail address is sgrager@ragerlaw.com.

Of her poem "Omega," Susan says, "this poem is a part of a continuing effort I am making in my poetry to really experience events and emotions with the high impact I imagine those happenings and sentiments have on those present at the time." Susan believes "Poetry can be autobiographical, of course, but that is necessarily a limited view from a single window. Poetry is a distillation of moments, a tuft of dreams, a tatter of memories, a collage crafted, glued, patched, and placed, with the intent that the tapestry is seamless."

Susan Godman Rager on the Web at Northern Neck of Virginia Law Page "Never undertake vast projects with half-vast ideas. . . ."

Ted Reynolds

Ted Reynolds claims, "The meaning is in the words of the poem. I don't analyze what I've written and I don't look back. Whatever it once was, is." Ted's many poems can be viewed at http://www.poets2000.com and http://netpoets.com. His e-mail is Tedrey@umich.edu.

Todd Michael St. Pierre

Todd Michael St. Pierre is primarily a children's author and a feature article/regular contributor for *Southern Living* and *Cooking Light Magazine.* His poem "Scattered Echoes" came about as a result of his own personal grief.

Gillian Savage

Gillian Savage lives in Sydney, Australia, with her husband and two teenage daughters. In a life of enquiry, she has sought to deepen her understanding of a spiritual life and stay true to its demands. She has been strongly influenced by the teaching of G. I. Gurdjieff, which emphasizes the need for active practice in daily life.

For her, poetry has been an important means of "facing the day." She finds that the struggle for effective expression of just what is can help to resolve and heal. She has seen that we are reshaped when we face difficulties that are too large for us. With help and effort, this reshaping is beneficial and we emerge stronger, simpler, and more humble. This reshaping is needed by the world. Her writing is presented on her Web site: www.tirralirra.com.

Sharon Swinney

Sharon Swinney lives near Brisbane, in Queensland, Australia with her husband David. They have been married for 17 years and have had 5 children, Emily – 10, Sarah – 9, Mary – deceased, Jack – 4, and Lucy – 2. Emily and Jack have Albinism, a hereditary condition that affects their vision and their sensitivity to sunlight.

Mary, their third child, was born with a Congenital Heart Defect and died when she was just 7½ weeks old. Sharon said, "Mary would have been 8 this year. Losing Mary is one of the hardest things I have ever had to cope with. It is a very long and difficult road to travel and it is one that, at times, you travel alone. Although others are grieving with you, everyone "lives" it differently. To try and cope with Mary's death, to try and have others understand what it feels like to lose your child, I started to write my feelings out as poems. They were put together in a book titled *From the Heart,* and are distributed by the Stillbirth and Neonatal Death Support (SANDS) organization in Australia.

For more of Sharon's poems visit her Web site for Mary at www.angelfire.com. To contact Sharon you can e-mail snowbrumby@hotmail.com.

Index

Made in the USA
Columbia, SC
06 May 2019